OCTOBER 1991!

ENJOY THE BEAUTY
AND FREEDOM OF OUR
NATION'S CAPITAL!

Enjoy the cultural and historical
diversity of the District!

Chris Batch

10-91

Looking west from the Library of Congress, into an early fall sunset, the dome of the Capitol glows in the wash of spotlights. In the distance, the Washington Monument, also bathed in light, reaches into the beautiful hues of the evening sky. These structures, more than any others, are the District's most enduring symbols.

Photo of Roger Miller

IMAGE PUBLISHING, LTD.

IMAGE PUBLISHING, LTD.
1411 Hollins Street/Union Square
301 · 566-1222   Baltimore, Maryland 21223   301 · 624-5253

DEDICATION

I am dedicating this book to my daughter, **Adrienne**. I can only hope that you grow up healthy, intelligent, strong and happy. It is my desire that I be as good a parent to you as my parents were to me. I want to teach and show you everything and, I find the more I do, the more I learn from you. Children are so wondrous, and I am so glad I have been able to experience this time with you. All my love, daddy.

Roger Miller, 5-4-91

Special thanks

I would like to thank everyone who had a part in this project. I would especially like to acknowledge the following:

A special thanks to all the people and businesses in Washington, D.C.. Without their hard work and dedication, Washington would not be the great city that it is today.

For their efforts and assistance from the very beginning, I would like to give my deepest thanks to **Linda Brown** and **Tom Murphy** at the Washington Convention and Visitors Association. I would also like to express my appreciation to **Dan Mobley** and **Marie Tibor** at the WCVA for their support.

A special thanks to the corporations and businesses who assisted us with the book through pre-publication purchases. Besides their commitments, their interest and advice were unexpected contributions of inestimable value.

I would like to thank everyone who gave of their hearts and minds and put forth great effort in getting photographs taken and information collected. To the many people who work at museums, galleries, historic sites and government offices in Washington, it shows you truly love your city.

A very special thanks to my close friend and associate **Chris Bohaska** for his time and cooperation in dealing with the pressures of creating our books.

A most sincere thanks to my parents, **Charles J.E. Miller** and **Ruth D. Miller**, for their continued patience, enduring spirit and unwavering belief in my work.

Roger Miller, 5-4-91

CREDITS

Photography by Roger Miller
Text by Chris Bohaska
Design by Roger Miller
Editing by Julie Schilling, Jan Watson, Chris Bohaska, Roger Miller
Typesetting and layouts by Delta Graphics, Inc., Peter Fernandez
Printing and Binding by Shiny Offset Printing Co. Ltd., Richard Ng, Hong Kong
Made in Hong Kong

INFORMATION

Library of Congress Catalog Number: 89-86032
ISBN: 0-911897-20-8

First Printing: 1991

ORDERS

For direct orders, please call or write for cost and shipping charges to the above address. Discounts are available for stores and institutions, minimum orders required.

Please note after November of 1991 area code will be changed to 410.

In an annual ritual of spring, cherry blossoms flower to full splendor, creating clouds of pink that fill the city with color. The Washington Monument rises majestically out of these pink clouds, reaching into the clear blue skies that announce the end of winter.

Spring is summoned in Washington with a burst of color. Cherry blossoms bloom as blue skies usher in the warm
air that allows sun-worshipers to paddle around the Tidal Basin in front of the Jefferson Memorial.
With thousands of acres of parks and waterways, Washington, D.C. rewards the wait through winter with
glorious natural and man-made wonders that are breathtaking and inspiring.

CONTENTS

Fireworks explode in streaks of vibrant colors over the Washington Monument on the Fourth of July. Millions visit Washington, D.C. each year, where Independence Day celebrations are best enjoyed in the atmosphere of the Mall. Many important national markers are illuminated by the dramatic light that marks the anniversary of the signing of the Declaration of Independence.

HISTORY

Washington, D.C. has always seemed like a magical city. Spacious museums, inspiring monuments and countless historic homes and buildings, in every imaginable architectural style, fill the landscape of blue waters and lush greenery that spread through the city. It's as if each structure, each tree, is meant to belong in its place, like pieces in a puzzle or stars in a complex galaxy.

After all, Washington is a unique capital. Unlike most national capitals, Washington was selected, planned and built with an artist's eye. Conceived as a permanent home for the federal government, the carefully rendered details also included plans for a city where Americans could forever celebrate their heritage. Some two hundred years later, walking around the Mall – past pools and fountains, in and out of museums and gardens, even on the steps of the Capitol – one is fully aware how the monuments, and the plan, celebrate the well-plotted story of this revolutionary nation. Surely, each monument, representing chapters in the history of the country, appeared like words on a page scribed effortlessly by some heavenly muse. It is as if they were born overnight, with lines of appreciative crowds waiting the next morning to share in the occasion of another historic event memorialized, another prominent American remembered.

Nothing, however, could be further from the truth. In fact, Washington, D.C. has a turbulent history of conflict and compromise – a history that is like a complex story woven with subplots and intrigue, with heroes and even a couple of villains. Like the concept of democracy itself, the District has grown out of differences, out of debate, through which change comes from the gradual consensus of many cultures and philosophies. And, as long as democracy survives, the city will continue to change and grow.

Soon after the Constitution was completed in 1787, the founding fathers set out to locate a site for a permanent national capital. Up through America's Revolutionary War years, the capital had moved from city to city along the Atlantic Coast, finally settling in Philadelphia. When the war ended, the country needed a permanent home for its national government. Like the process of forming a Constitution, the decision on locating the new capital city would result from debate and compromise. Northern factions, led by Alexander Hamilton, finally agreed to a plan set forth by Thomas Jefferson to locate the capital in the south in exchange for federal assumption of state debts that remained from the war. In 1790, Congress decided to meet in Philadelphia until 1800, with the idea of giving planners and architects ten years to prepare the new capital on the Potomac.

The first step commissioners took in forming the city was to name it "Washington," in honor of the first President. Chosen to oversee the selection of a site, George Washington decided upon Andrew Ellicott and his assistant Benjamin Banneker to survey a 100-square-mile tract just a few miles north of George Washington's home in Mount Vernon. Washington then selected a young Frenchman, Pierre L'Enfant, to be his chief engineer.

In 1791, L'Enfant presented Washington with an ambitious vision of the city. The prominent feature of the plan included focal points that coincided with the three major branches of government: the executive, legislative and judicial. Each branch was to be connected by major roads – literal and symbolic "avenues of communication" – in a complex, web-like pattern that coursed through the trees and marshes, symbolically reaching out to the common man whom the leaders of government served.

Jenkin's Hill, the city's highest elevation, was set aside for the Capitol: "a pedestal waiting for a monument," L'Enfant said. Designs were submitted. Thomas Jefferson, in a letter to L'Enfant in 1791, said he would "prefer the adoption of some one of the models of antiquity" for the Capitol, "and for the President's house, I should prefer the celebrated fronts of modern buildings." Whatever its appearance was to be, L'Enfant had set a spot for the President's house just a mile and a half northwest of the Capitol, almost in the center of the city. According to L'Enfant's layout, the house would be connected to the Capitol by a large avenue to allow easy access. The home of the judicial branch would be located somewhere in between the two, but away from major thoroughfares, symbolically isolated and uninfluenced by the politics of the president or Congress.

By the time Congress arrived for its first session in the new capital in 1800, little of L'Enfant's visionary plan was complete. L'Enfant had been relieved of his duties, many believe because of his arrogant attitude, with almost all the building in the city unfinished. Worse yet, the location for the city was proving to be far from pleasant. The air was hot and humid since most of the area was swampland. What roads existed were primitive, and turned muddy after early spring showers. Crossing the "avenues of communication" was a hazardous task. Mosquitoes buzzed and bit on summer evenings. Cattle and other livestock grazed on the grasses of the mall. One Congressman said the city was a place that "so many are willing to come to and all so anxious to leave." Because the city had grown almost out of an abyss, there was little or no business in the area to provide jobs for a stable economy. Without jobs, few people moved into the area. The ones who did were poor and survived in shantytown conditions. The Capitol and White House were still unfinished and the entire government, in 1802, accounted for only 291 persons, almost half of whom were congressmen.

A few years later, just as Washington began to show some potential, another dismal chapter opened on the city. In August of 1814, a British force invaded the city (its complex maze of roads proved indefensible), and set fire to the Capitol, the White House and other major public buildings. The Capitol and the White House were left as gutted shells. At the end of the war, Congress even voted on a measure to move the capital. It was defeated, but only narrowly. With new resolve, President Madison moved his offices to the Octagon House, and Congress convened for a while in the Patent Office. Slowly, the city began to rebuild and, at last, L'Enfant's famous plan began to be realized. Soon the city would be able to accept Charles Dickens' famous double-edged epithet, the "City of Magnificent Intentions."

The middle part of the 19th Century showed a series of triumphs and setbacks for the young capital. Although the Chesapeake and Ohio Canal (a planned waterway that many hoped would benefit commercial growth between Washington and the west) was an expensive failure, railroads and improved roads provided progressively better contact with surrounding areas. As the federal government's commitment to the area solidified, the commercial vitality of the city steadily grew. And, with these changes, the population grew.

But problems persisted through this time, also. Congress was often apathetic about the shortcomings of the city since representatives and senators returned to their home states soon after their sessions ended. The low point of this apathy was marked when Congress returned Alexandria to Virginia's jurisdiction in 1846 after minimal debate.

In one of the most common and dramatic views of the city, one can distinguish
L'Enfant's famous plan for the Mall from across the Potomac River. Three of the city's most important
structures – the Lincoln Memorial, the Washington Monument and the Capitol – come to life
in the lights of evening, like chess pieces lined up on a gameboard.

Furthermore, problems common to all cities remained troublesome. Fires were particularly devastating during the century because fire-fighting was inefficient and improperly handled. Sanitation was a problem, too. Ineffective waste removal and problems with the swampy wetlands caused an outbreak of Asiatic cholera in 1832 during which the mayor's wife, Marcia Burnes Van Ness, lost her life. The construction of the Washington Monument, begun in 1848, came to a halt in 1854 due to financial and political disagreements. Crime was a problem throughout all walks of life in the city, as even congressmen brawled on the floor of the House of Representatives. Ironically, it was to be America's darkest hours that actually kept the nation and the city intact.

By the time Abraham Lincoln arrived in Washington for his first inauguration in 1861, the southern states had begun secession, forming their own capital farther south. Among other problems, Lincoln would find the Capitol dome still unfinished and the Washington Monument no more than a stub rising from the marshes of the Potomac River. Because of its location, Washington was torn between the two sides of an impending Civil War. Holding the nation together meant holding the city together. In a letter to Horace Greeley, the editor of the "New York Tribune," Lincoln stated his prime purpose: "I would save the Union. The sooner the national authority can be restored, the nearer the Union will be `the Union as it was.'"

With soldiers cramming every space in the city, even the Capitol's Rotunda, Lincoln demanded that the dome of the Capitol be completed. "If people see the Capitol going on," he claimed, "it is a sign we intend the Union shall go on." The dome was finally completed in December 1863, and the city maintained order through the trying times. The Union victory in 1865 once again made Washington the sole capital of the nation.

Since that time, Washington has witnessed long periods of rapid growth. In 1871, Congress granted the District territorial status which spurred dramatic improvements in sanitary conditions and public works. Hundreds of dilapidated buildings were condemned, and new roads, sewers and sidewalks were laid out. Tens of thousands of trees were also planted all over the city. Although the improvements made during this time cannot be underestimated, corruption and graft was widespread, and the territorial government had to be abolished three years later in 1874.

In the 1880's and 90's, Washington saw a real estate boom that was unparalleled. Victorian mansions and opulent museums heralded the arrival of a social elite. Entertaining was sophisticated and commonplace. Even now, walking through elegantly preserved homes like the Christian Heurich mansion, one can't help but imagine the echoes of horse-drawn carriages on brick streets or the strains of string quartets resounding through gardens in summer.

It was during these years that Congress appropriated money to acquire the upper Rock Creek valley for a park, so the elite could enjoy their expanding leisure time on sunny afternoons. Picnics in the park, with women cavorting under parasols, men discussing business, and children running in the warm sun, were common sights on Sunday afternoons. In fall, rainbows of autumn hues materialized from the thick patches of trees that ran through the entire city. It was one of the city's grandest times.

The next marker of change in the city's history took place during World War I, when Washington's population exploded by 32 percent over the decade from 1910 to 1920. With Woodrow Wilson –the famed educator and statesman – leading the way, the nation took on an international role that was radically new. Huge numbers of government workers moved into the area. To some, the influx of new citizenry destroyed the intimate, southern-town charm of the city that so many loved. The pre-war city had relinquished its style to the crowded, impersonal feeling of the modern age. For others, though, that loss was more than compensated by the exciting new pace and intensity that signaled America's sudden prominence in the world.

The 1920's brought a tremendous wave of tourism along with an increase in population. The Lincoln Memorial was dedicated in 1922. The Smithsonian Institution, begun in 1855, was rapidly expanding. Concerts of classical music were held at the Library of Congress. Washington quickly took on the feel of a major cosmopolitan city during the "Jazz Age." It was in the '20's and '30's that the automobile also made its first impact on Washington. Not surprisingly, the city was plagued with traffic jams and accidents. Even a 22 mile-an-hour speed limit could not prevent some 9,400 accidents in 1925 alone, with traffic delays a common fact of life.

The Great Depression brought a construction boom in town, making the city seem almost depression-proof. The city felt that, like Lincoln's symbolic completion of the Capitol dome, completion of such landmarks as the Federal Triangle, the Supreme Court, the Longworth House Office Building and thousands of houses and apartments would show the nation the determined effort and leadership that originated in the capital. Much of what we see in Washington, D.C. today dates from this time.

The city saw a peak in its population through the forties, when World War II, like World War I, brought thousands to the city in support of the war effort. Talk with anyone who was in Washington at that time and you'll hear somber stories of war interwoven with joyous memories of a community spirit that existed throughout those turbulent years. Big band melodies were heard from jukeboxes and radios all over town as Americans banded together to win the war.

Since World War II, Washington has become a capital of world importance. Although population has steadily drifted from the city to the surrounding suburbs, Washington has seen rapid commercial growth over the last four decades. Construction in the city is booming, with new buildings replacing older, run-down structures at a surprising speed. Every time you visit the city, something is new. During the week, the pace is upbeat and hurried, as businessmen and – women rush to their next appointment, and tourists try to take in as much as they can. Weekends seem more relaxed, as joggers and frisbee tossers cross the mall with a sense of serious dedication to fun.

Through all the change and conflict, the city thrives. The monuments and museums, the galleries and sites, the acres upon acres of parks and grasslands still await any visitor searching for the history of a vital city, and of the nation that the city reflects and memorializes. Like passages in an ever-expanding history book, the monuments tell the story of a great land; a land that is a model of democracy for all nations. Walking up the sweeping steps of the Lincoln Memorial, one can feel the strength and dignity of this man who kept the Union together against great odds. Or, walking around the Tidal Basin in spring, with the blossoms of cherry trees filling the air, one can sense the vast intellect of Thomas Jefferson as he stands in the center of his beautifully rounded memorial. The Capitol, the source of symbols for many writers and leaders, stands as a beacon to the ideas and beliefs that this nation holds as self-evident for all.

Washington, D.C. has a long and fascinating history; a history that is interwoven with the nation's own. It is a history that reaches into the future, with dramatic new museums built underground, and new memorials that miraculously heal the tears and scars that the forces of history reveal. The pages of the city's history stand for all to read, for all to witness. And the future will be told in the granite and marble of monuments still to come.

From the observation windows high up in the Washington Monument, one can see the Mall's grassy expanse
stretching eastward to the Capitol. Across the horizon, spots of light emerge as dusk settles on the city, creating a
skyline of constellations in the blue illumination of evening. The sensitive lighting of Washington's monuments
and museums creates a different mood of the city from that conveyed in the daytime.

MONUMENTS

Washington, D.C. is a city of monuments; a place where we can trace the history of the nation and honor the people who have shaped that history. Sketched in the statues, columns and walls of the city's monuments are lessons of our common heritage, reminders of our most trying times, and a record of our most noble accomplishments.

Without a doubt, the most prominent of all the monuments in the District is the Washington Monument. From all over the city, one can see the white masonry obelisk that rises to touch the clouds, 556 feet above the Mall. Surrounded by a colonnade of American flags, fifty in all, the Washington Monument bears a fascinating history all its own.

Even while George Washington lived, plans were begun to build a magnificent memorial to honor the first president's vast contribution to the country. A National Monument Society was organized in 1833 to select a design for Washington's monument, and construction commenced soon thereafter. But persistent problems with funding, as well as chronic political bickering over details, caused work on the obelisk to come to a halt in 1854. By that time, the base of the monument stood on a small hill surrounded by swampland. It reached only 152 feet. Today, one can still see the subtle difference in color of the newer marble that was used when construction resumed well after the Civil War.

In 1884, a significantly enlarged monument was finally completed. It was worth the wait. Elevators now whisk passengers to the top of the monument, where a panoramic view, the best in the city, awaits. From here, Pierre L'Enfant's ambitious plan is breathtaking and fully realized. Looking to the east, visitors can gaze down the Mall, past the many museums and galleries, to the Capitol building. To the west, the Lincoln Memorial stands, doubled in the blue waters of the reflecting pool.

The memorial to Lincoln, a massive rectangular structure, stands in contrast to the vertical simplicity of the Washington Monument. Resembling a classical Greek temple, the memorial is a symbol of strength and dignity, qualities Lincoln summoned from the nation during America's darkest and most divided times. As the sun sets and shadows fall between its soaring marble columns, one can walk up the sweeping steps and behold the statue of Lincoln that sits inside, cast in a subtle, glowing light. The statue is modest, yet powerful, and captures the essence of Lincoln's steadfast spirit. That spirit is also rendered in the eloquent words of some of Lincoln's greatest writings, which are inscribed into the walls of the memorial.

Just footsteps away from the Lincoln Memorial, on the Tidal Basin, is the Jefferson Memorial, designed by John Russell Pope. Completed in 1942, the monument captures the Pantheon-style design that inspired Jefferson in his own plans for the University of Virginia and for his home, Monticello.

Often overlooked, the site of the Jefferson Memorial is one of great distinction. Located on the Tidal Basin, the Jefferson Memorial rests on a north-south line with the White House and the Washington Monument. With the Capitol and the Lincoln Memorial forming an east-west line, the Jefferson sits at the southern position in L'Enfant's plan for four major points which create a diamond-like border around the National Mall.

The beautiful circular colonnaded structure of the monument is a design which Jefferson is credited with having introduced to America. In early spring, when skies turn from grey to blue and warm breezes begin to drift through the city, one can stroll around the Tidal Basin with the Memorial as a focal point. The blossoms of Japanese cherry trees sweep around the monument, like circling clouds of pink, creating a flowing movement that blends with the monument's own circular structure. The statue inside depicts Jefferson as he stood before the committee appointed by the Continental Congress to compose the Declaration of Independence. Engraved on the interior walls are excerpts from works that hold Jefferson's beliefs on freedom, education, government and religion: beliefs that became the very fabric of the nation Jefferson helped to construct.

The newest national memorial is a few steps away from the Lincoln Memorial. Like the Lincoln, the Vietnam Memorial traces a complex period of American history. This monument honors not one man, but every American who perished in one of the country's longest wars. The names of the fallen are listed in the stone of the monument – the plain, unpretentious black marble panels that tear into the earth, deepening further and further as they document the progress of the war by year and by the number of casualties. Standing in front of it, catching one's own reflection in its mirroring shine, one becomes enveloped in the hush of a graveyard silence that softly speaks of the depth and solemnity of America's loss. Over the years, the monument has become a place of healing for America's veterans who feel its enigmatic power.

The other major structures in Washington, the White House and the Capitol, aren't monuments exactly, but they have certainly come to symbolize the essence of Washington just as the other monuments symbolize important events and personages.

The Capitol, with an evolutionary history that imitates that of the city itself, served as a symbol of continuity for Abraham Lincoln during the Civil War. With Union troops huddled in its Rotunda, Lincoln persuaded America to complete the dome, the spectacular centerpiece of the building: "If people see the Capitol going on," Lincoln said, "it is a sign we intend the Union shall go on."

Originally designed by William Thornton in the 1790's, the look of the Capitol has evolved dramatically, with expanded wings for the House and Senate along with two additional domes. The interior is filled with murals of famous historical scenes, and each state has been invited to contribute two statues of eminent Americans to Statuary Hall.

Through its many corridors, the congressional chambers and its massive Rotunda, the Capitol is an awe-inspiring site from any viewpoint. It is truly one of America's most enduring symbols.

The White House, the oldest public building in Washington, is another of the country's most lasting symbols. Although it has seen changes through the years, the building has managed to retain its understated beauty and remains one of Washington's most popular attractions. Centered amid 18 acres of serene gardens, fountains and greenery, the White House holds the stories of a succession of presidents who have contemplated the fate of the nation from within its walls.

America's legacy is captured in the splendor of Washington's monuments. In a city, and a country, that is ever-changing, it is no wonder that the monuments' many styles reflect that change and document its course. They lay out a map of where we've been, and invoke the proud history of a great land and a great people.

Whether seen from the Jefferson Memorial to the south, captured in the reflecting pool that
stretches west to the Lincoln Memorial, or from its base — with the sound of flags whipping in the wind –
the Washington Monument stands as a towering marker to one of the nation's greatest leaders.

With plans for a monument begun while George Washington was still alive,
the familiar obelisk has a tortured history of its own. It was not completed until 1884,
well after the Civil War, when it was the tallest building in the world. Still, at 556 feet high, with a colonnade of
flags encircling its base, the monument is a vertical focal point in a city of mostly horizontal lines.

Dedicated in 1943, and located on the south axis of the White House in L'Enfant's famous plan for the city,
the Jefferson Memorial holds one of the most prominent positions of all the monuments in the city.
On the four interior panels of the monument are inscriptions from some of Jefferson's most inspired writings on
freedom, education and democracy – all of which are cornerstones to the philosophy of the nation.

Author, statesman, scientist, inventor, Vice President, President, and educator, Thomas Jefferson was also a talented architect. His admiration for the circular dome of the Roman Pantheon – which he copied at the University of Virginia and at his home, Monticello – is reflected in the circular colonnaded structure of the Memorial. Appropriately, the classic style of the monument is one that Jefferson had introduced to America.

It's hard to believe that construction of the Jefferson Memorial once stirred controversy. Located on what had been a popular bathing beach, critics protested that its location was detrimental to the view of the Potomac. Others tied themselves to cherry trees to object to the erection of the monument. Today the memorial is a favorite among visitors, especially during Washington's Cherry Blossom Festival, which is held each spring.

With ground broken in 1939, the Jefferson Memorial became linked with a construction boom
that took place during Franklin Roosevelt's New Deal presidency.
Construction of the monument sent Americans a psychological message that the country would rise
out of the Great Depression with a new sense of optimism and pride.

"If people see the Capitol going on, it is a sign we intend the Union shall go on." So spoke Abraham Lincoln in the midst of the Civil War. The dome of the Capitol was indeed completed in late 1863, when it was crowned with the 19 1/2-foot Statue of Freedom. A symbol for Lincoln that the country would persist through its darkest hours, the Capitol building remains one of Washington's, and America's, most enduring symbols.

Considered a masterpiece of engineering, the Capitol is the dominating feature on the Mall
when viewed from any location. Originally designed by William Thornton in the 1790's,
the building has evolved and expanded dramatically past Thornton's relatively simplistic vision. Within, the
Capitol holds many grand spaces and chambers that reflect the dignity and grandeur of its purpose.

Pennsylvania Avenue comes alive at night with the lights of traffic in front of the Capitol.
One of the city's major thoroughfares, L'Enfant intended Pennsylvania Avenue to connect with President's home
with the chambers of the legislative branch at the Capitol. Recently, many of the historic structures
along this corridor have been restored and are enjoying a second life.

Filled with a maze of hallways and ornately decorated corridors,
the Capitol's interior highlights include a huge Rotunda that is filled with spectacular art work,
and Statuary Hall, where each state may contribute two statues of famous sons or daughters.

21

At the far west end of the Mall, the Lincoln Memorial stands over the reflecting pool with
an imposing sense of strength and dignity. Completed in 1922, the classical structure contains examples of
Lincoln's eloquent writings, including the Gettysburg Address and the Second Inaugural,
which are engraved on the interior walls of the monument.

Located in the center of the Lincoln Memorial, at the crest of its sweeping marble steps,
the sculpture of Abraham Lincoln looks east toward the Washington Monument and the Capitol. Sculpted by
Daniel Chester French, the stone captures Lincoln's unwavering dignity and his steadfast desire to
keep the divided nation united through its most perilous times.

Sitting amid 18 acres of greenery, the White House is surrounded by lush lawns dotted with trees and
well-kept gardens that lend a splash of color to the majestic home. Across Pennsylvania Avenue, to the north,
the White House looks out on Lafayette Park and the equestrian statue of Andrew Jackson.
At the corners of the park are four other statues, all honoring foreign-born Revolutionary War heroes.

Looking down on the White House from the Hay-Adams Hotel, one sees the proximity of the
Washington Monument and Jefferson Memorial. Though the influences of each president since Jefferson
and Adams can be seen at the White House, the structure retains its original beauty.
Reminiscent of an 18th Century country house, the White House has been home to American presidents
since John and Abigail Adams moved in in 1800.

With the name of every American killed in the Vietnam War engraved on its black granite panels,
the Vietnam Veterans Memorial has come to symbolize many things for many people.
One symbol is as a temple of mourning, and reconciliation, that has a unique and powerful effect on
each individual that walks its length. Every day, hundreds of people leave wreaths, notes, flowers and
pictures on the tombstone-like monument in remembrance of friends and family.

Dedicated in late 1982, the Vietnam Veterans Memorial is designed to be deceptively simple.
Shaped like an open book, its panels reveal the history of the war, without moral or political prejudice.
Just as it reflects the image of each person who looks at it, the meaning and importance of the Memorial comes
from within those who experience it. One magazine called it "the most emotional ground in the nation's capital."

Stepping into the Christian Heurich Mansion is like stepping into the Gilded Age,
when Washington saw a real estate boom that forever changed the city. Christian Heurich, a local brewer,
built the house in 1894 and filled it with Victorian appointments, which the Washington Historical Society now
maintains as a museum. The Washington Historical Society meets regularly and offers fascinating
information on the city's architectural and cultural history.

HISTORIC SITES

To really "feel" a city's history, to make the words in history books come alive, one can do no better than to visit the sites where historic events transpired. Washington, D.C. is no exception. The District's history is especially rich with handsomely restored homes and landmarks that function like time machines, where one can capture the life and spirit of eras past.

George Washington's home, Mount Vernon, stands just a few miles south of the city on the shores of the Potomac. The meticulously landscaped lawns of this gleaming white plantation invoke the passion for balance and order that the 18th century gentleman farmer strove to maintain. Inside, a secretary-desk looks over the modest furnishings of the study, where Washington composed many of the letters that were concerned with the construction of the city itself.

Also located in Virginia, just outside of the city, is the Arlington National Cemetery. The final resting place of many national heroes and celebrities, as well as the location of the Tomb of the Unknowns, much of the land here was once owned by Mrs. Robert E. Lee. The Arlington House, on the grounds, is now a memorial to General Lee, who lived here for thirty years before the beginning of the Civil War. North, toward Rosslyn, is the Iwo Jima Memorial, which commemorates the service of American Marines who have died defending the United States.

In historic Georgetown, among the traffic and window-shoppers, one can seek out the time before the Revolution at the Old Stone House, located on M Street. Begun in 1764 by Christopher Layman, the Old Stone House is believed to be the oldest house in the District. Meander along the stone path that twists through the garden on the house's north end and step into a faraway time when Washington was a sleepy little village, straining with the growing pains of commerce and politics.

A block from the White House is the Octagon House, where President Madison signed the Treaty of Ghent that ended the War of 1812. Madison moved into the Octagon in September 1814 after the British had raided Washington and set the Capitol and White House afire. Built in the 1790's, the home was the social center of Washington for years. Early sketches reveal that it was situated on open expanses of farmland, even though it stood just a block away from the President's House. In recent years the home has been carefully restored. Once the headquarters for The American Institute of Architects, the current offices for the A.I.A are located next door.

Also a block from the White House is the home of one of the War of 1812's heroes, Stephen Decatur. The Decatur House, located on Lafayette Square, was built in 1816 but was occupied by the Decaturs for only 14 months. After Decatur was mortally wounded in a duel, his wife, Susan Decatur, left the property to a succession of distinguished tenants. In 1871, it was purchased by the Beale family. The Beales added Victorian touches to the mansion, like gaslights, floral painted ceilings and dramatic parquet flooring. Restored by the National Trust for Historic Preservation, the house offers many distinctive examples of Federal and Victorian architecture. And, just a few blocks from the Decatur House, down 17th Street, one will find the DAR Museum and Constitution Hall.

Many historic sites in Washington, D.C. are living museums-buildings which continue to be used for either their original purposes, or for new functions. For example, Pierce Mill, in Rock Creek Park, has been restored to its original splendor, and grains are again being ground for flour with the help of waterpower from Rock Creek.

Waterpower is also a major attraction at Great Falls Park, where the Potomac rushes violently over mammoth rocks that cut through the river. On the Maryland side of the falls, the Great Falls Tavern acts as a Visitor's Center at the C&O Canal Historical Park. Originally intended as a commercial route to the Ohio Valley, the C&O Canal currently attracts hikers, joggers, canoeists and nature lovers with miles of serene, wooded terrain.

Massive houses like the Meridian House and White-Meyer House, once the homes and social centers for some of the city's most eminent families, still operate today as locations for social and business functions. Walking through these stately mansions, or into the formal gardens outside, one can confront the intimate surroundings where business and power was, and still is, discussed.

Two homes that display a vast difference of styles are the Clara Barton House and the Christian Heurich Mansion. The Clara Barton House, in Glen Echo, Maryland, was used for a while as a Red Cross headquarters, and it retains the understated simplicity of a woman who dedicated her life to comforting others. The Red Cross Headquarters are currently housed in a Georgian-style mansion near the White House.

The Christian Heurich Mansion, home of the prominent businessman and brewer, is an opulent treat of ornate Victorian architecture and decorative arts. The thirty-one room home, current headquarters of the Historical Society of Washington, D.C., reflects the grandeur of the Gilded Age – a time when Washington's elite boldly displayed the lavish fruits of their labors.

Another impressive home is the Anderson House, located in the Dupont Circle area. Built in 1905 by career diplomat Larz Anderson, the house is filled with European and Oriental antiques and art that Anderson collected during his tenure as an ambassador. In 1937, Anderson left the house and his collections to the Society of Cincinnati, an organization for officers of the Continental Army which was founded in 1783. Today, the Society is composed of their descendants, and it displays artifacts commemorating the American Revolution and its commander, George Washington.

Also in Dupont Circle, on S Street, is the Woodrow Wilson House. The famed educator and diplomat is the only U.S. President to have retired in Washington, D.C.

One of the most haunting sites in town, The Ford's Theatre, is also a living museum. Built in 1863, Ford's is the site where Abraham Lincoln was fatally wounded shortly after his second inaugural. Carried to the Petersen House across the street, Lincoln died the next morning in a tiny back bedroom. The Ford's Theatre has been restored and is again a living theatre operating with a full schedule. Also a museum to Lincoln, the theatre's details correspond faithfully to the way they were on that fateful night.

Black abolitionist Frederick Douglas, a contemporary of Lincoln's, lived in the beautiful Victorian house on Cedar Hill, in Anacostia, from 1877 to 1895. On display here are exhibits that describe the life of a man who was born into slavery but who would later become a spokesman for his people.

The National Cathedral, begun in 1907, was just recently completed. Sitting among acres of wooded land, the National Cathedral is a temple for all faiths. One of the largest Gothic cathedrals in the world, its 14th century-styled spires can be seen from many vantage points in the city.

One doesn't need to learn history simply through books – Washington has a living history, waiting for anyone who can imagine their own journey through time. Washington's rich heritage is an exciting journey through the gardens and the hallways of its historic buildings; a journey that captures the diverse personalities and vast changes the city has witnessed.

The Anderson House, located near Dupont Circle, was built in 1906 for Larz Anderson, the American ambassador to Japan. This grand mansion now displays Anderson's collection of European and Oriental decorative arts. The Society of Cincinnati, a patriotic organization dating to the Revolution, also has a museum here, where it displays memorabilia relating to the Revolutionary War and its commander, George Washington.

The only former president to make his home in the nation's capital, Woodrow Wilson retired to this stately home
on S Street in the 1920's. The red-brick Georgian Revival house, through the National Trust for
Historic Preservation, protects the artifacts of the president who expanded America's role in the world
during his multi-faceted career as historian, educator, statesman and president.

Decatur House

Octagon House

DAR Constitution Hall

Octagon House

Three historic properties located near the White House are the Decatur House, Octagon House and DAR
Constitution Hall. The Octagon House is where President Madison lived after the British burned the White House
in the War of 1812. One of that war's heroes, Stephen Decatur, lived for a while in the Lafayette Square structure,
dating from 1819. Constitution Hall is the headquarters for the Daughters of the American Revolution,
and includes an auditorium, a library, and a museum.

Meridian House International

White-Meyer House

Meridian House International

Meridian House International

A time of elegant homes in the District is reflected in the beautiful architecture of the Meridian House
and White-Meyer House. Both homes now display art and furnishings of worldwide interest.
They are also available for banquets and meetings, with the spectacular gardens being especially
popular locations. The Meridian House International Organization promotes international understanding
through cultural exchange, with programs for organizations with international concerns.

Frederick Douglas National Historic Site

Old Stone House

Pierce Mill

Old Stone House

The Frederick Douglas house, located in Cedar Hill, displays 90 percent of the black abolitionist's original possessions. Pierce Mill, a 19th century grain mill in Rock Creek Park, is an operational site, using water power from Rock Creek. The Old Stone House features costumed tour-guides who describe life before the Revolution.

The Old Stone House is believed to be the oldest home in Washington, D.C.
Located in historic Georgetown, and built in 1765, tours at the house present a glimpse into life as it was
lived in the 18th century. The garden, on the north end of the house, is laden with flowers
that were common in the district during a slower-paced era.

Memorial Amphitheater

Tomb of the Unknowns

Arlington House or Custis-Lee Mansion

Arlington National Cemetery

Overlooked by the Custis-Lee Mansion, or Arlington House,
the pre-Civil War home of Robert E. Lee, is Arlington Cemetery. Rows and rows of tombstones mark
the resting place of nearly 200,000 members of the military. Guards keep 24 hour vigil at the
Tomb of the Unknowns, which honors soldiers from all of America's wars. Numerous veteran and
civic groups hold services at the Memorial Amphitheater, also located on the grounds.

Looking past one of the locks on the Chesapeake and Ohio Canal, one can look down the tree-lined waterway into a bygone time when Americans believed the canal would be a major source of commerce between Washington and Pittsburgh. Ground-breaking ceremonies took place in 1828, but railroads soon made the canal obsolete. Today, the canal acts as a romantic backdrop to the historical Georgetown area.

Clara Barton House

American Red Cross Headquarters

Peterson House

Three historic sites in Washington include the Red Cross Building, the House Where Lincoln Died and the
Clara Barton House. The Clara Barton House, located just north of Washington, D.C., in Glen Echo,
allows examination of the complex character of one of America's greatest humanitarians. Once a headquarters
for the American Red Cross, the current headquarters are located on 17th Street near the White House.

Built in 1861 by John T. Ford, the Ford's Theatre has had a turbulent history of fire and closings.
Its place in history is cemented, though, as the theatre where Abraham Lincoln was shot in 1865.
Lincoln was carried across the street from the theatre and eventually died in the Peterson House
(preceding page, right). Fully restored during several stages in the 20th century, Ford's Theatre is now a
museum to Lincoln as well as an active theatre featuring contemporary American plays.

One of the largest Gothic cathedrals in the world, the stained glass windows
of the National Cathedral cast multi-colored light on the exquisite masonry work of the interior.
Subtle shades of light are cast throughout the cathedral, which is a temple intended for all faiths.
It also contributes to the cultural life of the city by sponsoring many forms of artistic performance.

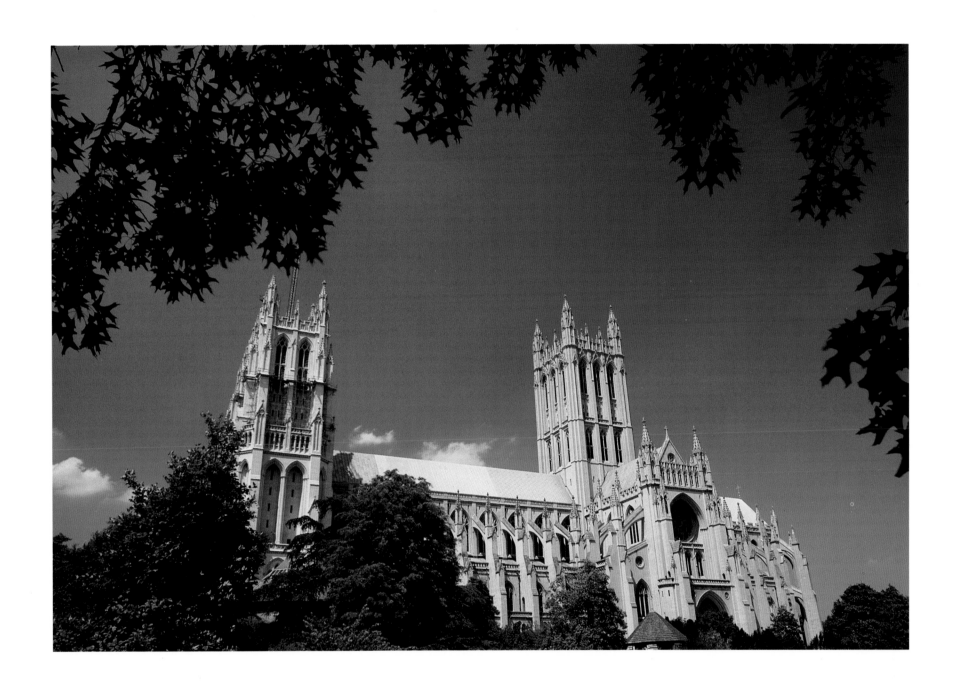

The National Cathedral, reflecting the monumental style of 14th century European cathedrals,
rises out of fifty-seven acres of trees and greenery on the northwest side of town.
Begun over eighty years ago, when President Theodore Roosevelt laid the foundation stone in 1907,
the Gothic Cathedral was completed and dedicated in September 1990.

The Marine Corps War Memorial, better know as the Iwo Jima Statue, is dedicated to the memory
of all the Marines who have died in America's wars. Located just north of Arlington Cemetary,
the statue is based on the famous photograph taken by Joe Rosenthal of troops raising the American flag
after capturing Mount Suribachi in the battle of Iwo Jima during World War II.

Located south of the city, on the Potomac River in Virginia, George Washington's famed
Mount Vernon estate remains essentially unchanged since he lived there. It was from here that
Washington supervised the site selection and the plans for the Capital city.
Its 8,000 acre site has been maintained for years by the Mount Vernon Ladies' Association.

Overlooking the Enid A. Haupt Garden, the "Castle" was the Smithsonian Institution's first building.
Designed by James Renwick, Jr., and completed in 1855, the unique sandstone structure displays several styles
of towers, or turrets, that can be seen from all over the Mall. Now an administrative building,
the Castle best symbolizes the extensive collection that is often called "the Nation's Attic."

MUSEUMS

In 1800, when the U.S. Congress moved from Philadelphia to Washington, D.C., $5,000 was appropriated to purchase books for a library to serve the needs of the legislators. From that point, nearly two hundred years ago, the Library of Congress has grown to almost inconceivable proportions. The largest library in the world, it contains over 85 million items, with over 31,000 new books, periodicals and recordings arriving every day.

The staggering growth seen at the Library of Congress is mirrored by that of many of the museums and libraries located in and around the nation's capital. The District is a curiosity-seeker's paradise, where everything under the sun, and then some, can be looked at, opened up or tracked down.

Like many of the city's museums, the Library of Congress had humble beginnings. Originally located in the Capitol, the collection went up in flames when the British set the town afire in 1814. When President Thomas Jefferson sold his extensive book collection as a replacement, the library immediately became the largest single collection in the nation. In 1897, officials were forced to build a massive structure to house the growing accumulation of books, charts, maps, photographs, prints, recordings and musical compositions. Since then, two new buildings have been added, the latest of which, the James Madison Memorial Building, is the largest single library building in the world.

Another huge collection of documents is located at the National Archives. Probably best known for its Rotunda, where the Declaration of Independence, the Constitution and the Bill of Rights are displayed, the National Archives preserves and makes available billions of records relating to the history of the nation and of the federal government.

Completed in 1937, the National Archives is the ideal place to trace your genealogy, or to research aspects of American history. With operations in fifteen states, the National Archives and Records Administration provides regional research facilities that include fourteen record centers and eight Presidential libraries. In Washington, a trip to the National Archives' massive Rotunda for a look at America's most precious documents is a great starting place for a tour of the city.

Finding a starting place to explore the Smithsonian Institution, Washington D.C.'s most renowned and extensive collection of museums and galleries, is just about impossible. There's just too much to see. Established through a bequest of $550,000 to the United States from Englishman James Smithson, the Institution's first structure, commonly known as "The Castle," was completed in 1855. The red-brick building, designed by architect James Renwick, Jr., has come to symbolize the collection that is often called "the Nation's Attic."

Originally planned as a center for research and learning, the Smithsonian accepted an expanded vision when the Philadelphia Centennial Exhibition of 1876 was moved to the Arts & Industries building, located next to the Castle. When Congress appropriated money to form a "National Museum," the Smithsonian grew into a complex of exhibits and popular events that now includes over a dozen museums and galleries covering cultural, scientific, technological and artistic contributions from all over the world.

Across the Mall from the Castle is the National Museum of American History. Built in 1964, its exhibits capture the essence of America's past. Here you'll find displays on diverse subjects, like the gigantic, 1920's Southern Railway locomotive, a classic Packard Phaeton, or a display of American First Ladies' gowns. Stamp and coin enthusiasts can spend hours searching through rare collections from times past. Others may stand in awe of the original Star-Spangled banner that flew over Fort McHenry and inspired the writing of the National Anthem.

Next door to the Museum of American History is one of the Smithsonian's most popular collections, the National Museum of Natural History. Here you can find treasures such as dinosaur bones dug from the depths of the earth or rocks dug from the surface of the moon. With displays varying from insects to beautiful gems to birds and mammals, the Museum of Natural History strives for and succeeds at displaying the cultural and natural history of mankind and his home, the earth.

Back on the other side of the mall is one of the newest attractions, and the most visited. The National Air and Space Museum displays aircraft and spacecraft in a huge structure that allows the planes to hang overhead, reflecting their original grandeur as they seemingly race through the sky. Here you'll trace the history of flight, from the Wright Brothers' plane to the Spirit of St. Louis; from the Gemini rockets to an Apollo lunar module that landed on the moon. And, at the Albert Einstein Planetarium, you'll be able to lift off into space, exploring about 9,000 stars and the motion of the sun, the moon and five planets on the Planetarium's 70-foot dome.

If you wish to stay rooted to this world, one can visit the National Geographic Society's Explorers Hall, where a gigantic model of the globe is just one of many exhibits that teaches us about the fascinating aspects of the earth and its environment.

South and east of the Mall, in the Washington Naval Yard, one can visit the Navy Museum and the U.S.S. Barry. A tribute to naval fighting ships, the Navy Museum is located in a former warehouse and describes America's naval history with models and artifacts of our finest ships and aircraft. Across the Anacostia River, the Anacostia Museum proudly exhibits the contributions of African Americans. Illustrating African American culture and history, the Anacostia Museum has exhibited work from subjects as varied as the Harlem Renaissance to the development of African American churches.

The National Zoo, located in Woodley Park, makes available the study of a subject for children of all ages: animals. Lots of them. Probably best known for their giant pandas, the National Zoo has more than 3,500 animals of over 500 different species. Although it may seem that the zoo exists for fun and childhood delights, studies at the National Zoo are part of an international effort to protect and preserve threatened species. Part of the Smithsonian network, the Zoo makes an important impact on our ecological community.

Two other museums in Washington study and display flora and fauna. The U.S. Botanic Gardens, on the Mall just west of the Capitol, exhibits rare plants and flowers from all over the world in a exotic setting of glass and stone buildings. And the U.S. National Arboretum features flora that fill 444 acres of open parkland along New York Avenue. One of the most fascinating exhibits at the Arboretum is a collection of bonsai trees, some of which are over three centuries old.

Washington is an international center of cultural and historical wealth. Museums offer a multitude of displays and exhibits that touch on all aspects of the earth's, and man's, creations. Explore even a minute part of it, and one is sure to come away with new ideas and new perspectives on our place in the world.

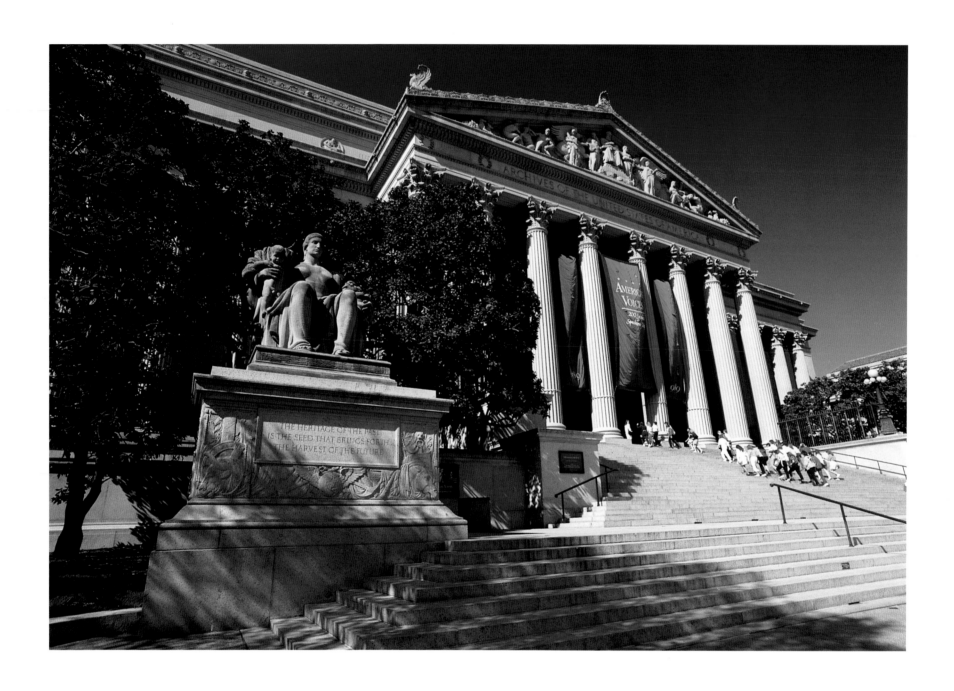

The National Archives is the home of some of America's most meaningful documents. Most famous of these documents are the Declaration of Independence, the Constitution and the Bill of Rights, which are displayed in the Rotunda. They are protected in helium-filled bronze cases that are raised from a 50-ton vault for all to see.

The National Archives preserves and makes available for reference billions of documents,
maps and photographs as well as millions of feet of film. Thousands of shelves of books, providing information
on all aspects of American history, are permanently stored at many locations across the United States.
Document restoration is also a crucial part of the work done at the National Archives.

Displaying treasures from the past, the National Museum of Natural History is one of Washington's most popular sites. Famous for its vast array of dinosaurs, the museum also houses a seemingly infinite collection of plant and sea life, rocks and minerals, and even meteorites from the far reaches of the solar system.

The size of the collection at the Museum of Natural History increases by up to a million new
specimens a year. The exhibits gathered here attempt to describe millions of years of life on earth and the
secrets of millions of miles of outer space. The museum also explains the diversity of nature as well
as the variety of cultures all over the world.

On display at the Air and Space Museum are artifacts from America's pioneering space program,
including Skylab, the Apollo 11 Command Module and a touchable moon rock. Along with these space age
displays, the museum also offers a planetarium, where visitors can explore the complex mechanics
and puzzling mysteries of the universe.

In a celebration of flight, and ultimately to the power of the imagination,
the National Air and Space Museum has become one of Washington, D.C.'s most visited attractions.
Historic planes, like the Wright flyer and the Spirit of St. Louis, appear to soar through the air above,
as they describe the highest altitudes of mankind's greatest achievements.

The Arts and Industries Museum, the second oldest Smithsonian building,
stands on the Mall next to the Smithsonian Castle. Capturing the spirit of a rapidly growing
America of the 19th Century, the Arts and Industries Building features the Baldwin Locomotive and
a fascinating collection of North American Indian totem poles.

Home to more than 3,500 animals of 500 different species, the National Zoological Park is probably
best known for its cuddly Giant Pandas, which were gifts from the People's Republic of China. Surrounded
by the lush greenery of Rock Creek Park, the Zoo is also a world center for the study of threatened species.

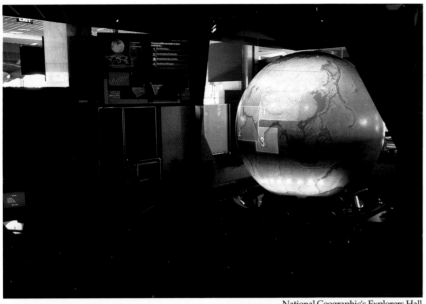

National Geographic's Explorers Hall

Anacostia Museum

Navy Museum

U.S.S. Barry

Important museums in Washington include Explorers Hall, which boasts a huge globe of the
earth displaying information on weather and environmental concerns. The Anacostia Museum, part of the
Smithsonian Institution, describes various cultural and artistic contributions of African Americans.
The Navy Museum and the U.S.S. Barry chronicle the history of the Navy from the Revolution to the present.

The United States flag that flew over Fort McHenry during the War of 1812,
and inspired the National Anthem, hangs in the National Museum of American History.
The museum, which embodies the nation's technological and cultural heritage, also highlights the John Bull
locomotive, Ford's Model T and Alexander Graham Bell's original experimental telephone.

U.S. Botanic Gardens

U.S. Botanic Gardens

National Arboretum

U.S. Botanic Gardens

Exotic flora and fauna from around the world are studied and displayed in lush surroundings at the
U.S. Botanic Gardens and the National Arboretum. The Botanic Gardens has a history that stretches back to the
early 1800's when travelers returned to the U.S. with plants and flowers for a museum.
One of the major exhibits at the Arboretum is a display of bonsai trees, some of which are over 350 years old.

The U.S. National Arboretum stretches out along New York Avenue and fills over 444 acres of land. Over 70,000 azaleas, rhododendrons, hollies and various species of trees are displayed here. There is also a National Herb Garden, as well as numerous examples of colorful flowers, like these water lilies. One of the Arboretum's most popular exhibits is the National Bonzai Collection, which features dozens of miniature trees.

Originally housed in what is now the Renwick Gallery, the Corcoran Gallery moved
to its present location on 17th Street and New York Avenue in 1897. The collection is exhibited in
surroundings that are bold and beautiful. Its current building, designed in the Beaux Arts style,
features mostly great works of American painting and sculpture.

THE ARTS

Looking at tour books and pamphlets, one may not realize that appellations like Smithson, Corcoran, Hirshhorn, Phillips or Mellon are more than just the names of local galleries and museums. These names belong to just a few of the great philanthropists who have blessed Washington, D.C. with gifts and collections that have made the city one of the greatest art centers of the world.

Long known as the Andrew Mellon Gallery, the National Gallery of Art, begun with Mellon's bequest of 13th to 19th century masterworks, has grown rapidly. A second structure, the East Building, had to be constructed in 1978 in order to house the ever expanding collection. The new wing's design, modern-looking and trapezoidal in shape, stands in sharp contrast to the domed, neo-classical structure that houses the original collection. Appropriately, the West Building holds primarily great European works by artists like da Vinci, Rembrandt and Monet, in over 100,000 square feet of exhibition space. The East Building, on the other hand, displays works by important twentieth century artists like Pollock, Mondrian and Henry Moore.

The National Gallery is just one of many galleries connected with the Smithsonian Institution's network of museums. Another Smithsonian museum is the National Museum of American Art. With over 34,000 paintings, sculptures, graphics, folk art and photographs, the Museum of American Art is located in the Old Patent Office building several blocks north of the National Mall. The collection includes work from America's colonial times to the present, by artists as varied as Thomas Hart Benton and Robert Rauschenberg.

Also located in the Old Patent Office building is the National Portrait Gallery. The concept of a portrait gallery is as old as the city itself: Pierre L'Enfant's original plan for the District included a pantheon for the nation's most prominent citizens. The history of America, through portraiture, is documented at the Portrait Gallery by thousands of diverse works, including a collection of *Time* magazine covers, photographs of baseball heroes, and portraits of Americans ranging from Pocahontas to George Bush.

Still we haven't scratched the surface. Museums dedicated to Asian and African culture and art are newcomers on the block. Built underground on the Mall, the Arthur Sackler Gallery and the National Museum of African Art act as twin museums that offer glimpses of civilizations vastly different than our own. Through these museums, we have valuable artifacts of religious and cultural importance that show us how distant societies live and worship.

Not all of the city's museums are as vast as these, but all do offer insights into the inestimable contributions made by members of the national community. The National Museum of Women In The Arts, for instance, demonstrates the vast heritage of art conceived and nurtured by women, in a setting that conveys the dignity and grace of an often overlooked segment of the artistic population.

The Renwick Gallery, part of the National Museum of American Art, exhibits a variety of 20th century American crafts and decorative arts. Designed by James Renwick, the architect who designed the Smithsonian Castle, the gallery was originally built for William Corcoran to accommodate his extensive collection of American art. The Corcoran Gallery of Art was eventually moved, and the Renwick, located across the street from the White House, was restored in the 1960's. Many of the Renwick's rooms and galleries, like the Grand Salon and the Octagon Room, are arranged to show off not just fine painting and sculpture, but also the furnishing styles of some of the city's art collectors and philanthropists of the 1860's and '70's.

The Corcoran Gallery of Art, now located west of the White House on 17th Street, specializes in American painting and sculpture. William Wilson Corcoran, a banker and financier, was particularly interested in collecting American paintings of the 18th and 19th centuries. Today, some of this nation's greatest works of art are displayed in the stately surroundings of the Corcoran's majestic structure. Designed in the Beaux Arts style, the Corcoran building is considered an architectural masterpiece that is as impressive as the artwork it shelters. The Corcoran is also the home of one of America's most prestigious art schools.

One of the newest museums, as well as one of the most dramatic in appearance, is the Hirshhorn Museum and Sculpture Garden. Located on the Mall, the giant cylindrical-shaped museum opened in 1974. Created from a bequest by financier Joseph H. Hirshhorn, the museum displays a comprehensive collection of modern painting and sculpture. Exhibits at the Hirshhorn capture the newest trends in contemporary art by both individuals and schools of artists. It is not the first museum in Washington to do so; the Hirshhorn continues a tradition begun in this nation by collector Duncan Phillips, who was responsible for initiating the Phillips Collection.

Located near Dupont Circle, the Phillips Collection was the first museum in the U.S. dedicated to modern art. Created in 1921, and originally composed of only two rooms in Phillips' home, the collection shows the work of artists who attempted to "break the mold," and propel the art world into new directions. Although the collection has grown rapidly, the museum still maintains Phillips' original dream of displaying visionary work in dignified and intimate settings.

Not all of Washington's art life is confined to painting and sculpture; the city has a rich tradition of theatre and music that is also unsurpassed. Best known among the city's theatres is the Kennedy Center for the Performing Arts, which stretches along the Potomac River in Foggy Bottom. Opened in 1971, the center celebrates a variety of performing arts including theatre, opera, dance, symphony and film. The Kennedy is the home of the American Film Institute and the Washington Opera, as well as the place where the National Symphony Orchestra performs.

The oldest continually-run theatre in the city, the National Theatre, is located on E Street in Downtown. Within the historic Pennsylvania Avenue district, it was recently renovated and enjoys a rich theatrical heritage.

On Capitol Hill, the Folger Shakespeare Theatre presents plays by Shakespeare and his contemporaries in an Elizabethan setting. The Folger Library, completed in 1932, holds the largest collection of Shakespeare's works in the world, as well as extensive holdings of other Renaissance materials.

And, just outside the city, in Vienna, Virginia, is Wolf Trap Farm. An open air facility, Wolf Trap presents entertainment ranging from music to puppet shows from summer to autumn.

Washington has been blessed with a number of devoted philanthropists whose collections and bequests have enhanced the cultural atmosphere of the city. Through people like James Smithson and Duncan Phillips, Washington's galleries and theatres are able to make art available to all. For research, or just for passing time on a Sunday afternoon, everyone will find enjoyment and inspiration in the galleries and museums throughout the city.

West Building

East Building

West Building

East Building

The National Gallery of Art, created through a bequest by art collector Andrew Mellon,
has one of the most comprehensive collections of European and American art in the world. The East Building,
with its brash angular surfaces and striking interior spaces, includes masterpieces of 20th century painting
and sculpture by artists like Picasso, Matisse, Pollock and Modigliani.

The classic West Building of the National Gallery of Art includes the spectacular rotunda
that is the centerpiece of the structure designed by John Russell Pope. Housing paintings, sculpture and
graphic arts from the 13th century to the present, the gallery exhibits the finest accumulation of European art
in the United States. Included in the collection is the "Ginevra de' Benci,"
the only painting by Leonardo da Vinci outside of Europe.

Just off the Mall, the National Museum of American Art houses over 34,000 paintings, sculptures and other works of art in a setting that is a work of art in itself. The country's oldest national art collection, with works by artists as diverse as Thomas H. Benton, Winslow Homer, Thomas Cole and Robert Rauschenberg, shares space in the Old Patent Office building with the National Portrait Gallery.

Home to the "Hall of Presidents," the Meserve gallery of Mathew Brady photographs,
and a collection of "Time" magazine covers, the National Portrait Gallery boasts a gigantic gathering of
portraits of people who possess a special place in American history. The Old Patent Office Building, a towering
Greek Revival structure, houses this collection, as well as the National Museum of American Art.

The Hirshhorn Museum and Sculpture Gallery's controversial cylindrical-shaped structure
is 231 feet in diameter and sits on four massive piers, 14 feet above the ground. Begun from Joseph H. Hirshhorn's
art collection and bequest of one million dollars, the museum includes over 2,000 sculptures set in the museum,
its plaza and its distinctive sunken sculpture garden.

Exhibits at the Hirshhorn Museum and Sculpture Garden capture the newest
trends in contemporary art, as well as the history of painting and sculpture of the past century.
With over 13,000 paintings, sculptures and works on paper, the Hirshhorn contains one of the
world's most comprehensive collections of modern art.

The John F. Kennedy Center for the Performing Arts, located in Foggy Bottom,
stretches out along the Potomac in the violet hues of twilight. With several grand halls and theatres,
the Kennedy Center accommodates the National Symphony Orchestra, the Washington Opera and the
American Film Institute, as well as some of the area's finest performances in opera, music, film, drama and dance.

The glorious Opera House, one of the halls at the Kennedy Center,
is the stately setting for performances of opera and ballet. Opened in 1971, the center had been planned for years.
After Kennedy's death in 1963, it was dedicated as a living memorial to the slain president. Sixty nations from
around the world honored Kennedy's memory with precious gifts that now grace the center.

Wolf Trap Farm for the Performing Arts

Folger Shakespeare Theatre

National Museum of African Art

Arthur Sackler Gallery

Two new museums located underground on the Mall are the Sackler Gallery
and the National Museum of African Art. The Museum of African Art describes many cultural and religious
facets of sub-Saharan societies through arts and crafts made from a variety of materials.
Local theatres include the Folger Shakespeare Theatre, where performances of Shakespeare and his
contemporaries are held. Wolf Trap Farm, an open-air facility, is located in suburban Virginia.

The Arthur Sackler Gallery features a fascinating collection of ancient and contemporary art work
that describes the cultural history of the Middle East, the Far East and Southeast Asia. Located near the
Smithsonian Castle, the Sackler's structure mirrors that of the Museum of African Art.
Large rooms are highlighted with displays of beautiful craftwork, sculpture and religious icons.

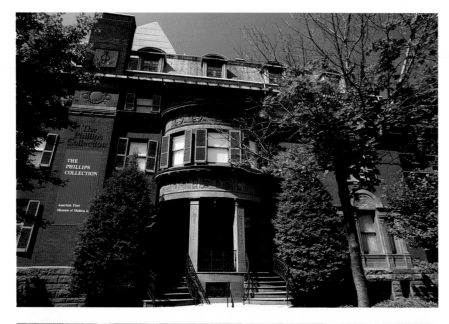

Originally only two large rooms in a private home near Dupont Circle,
the Phillips Collection was the first museum of modern art in the country. Since its inception,
the collection has swiftly expanded to include 2,500 works of spectacular art work.
Despite the rapid growth, the Phillips Collection has been able to maintain Duncan Phillips' original
desire to keep the museum's dignity and intimacy intact.

The National Museum of Women in the Arts, located on New York Avenue,
collects a comprehensive survey of women's art from the 16th century to the present.
The beautiful marble walls and columns in the Renaissance Revival structure create the perfect backdrop
for work by important artists like Fontana, Ruysch and Cassatt.

Part of the National Museum of American Art, the Renwick Gallery exhibits
the important achievements of designers and craftspeople of the United States in intimate,
richly appointed surroundings. The Gallery displays a vast variety of distinctly American works
that celebrate the country's rich history and diversity in the decorative arts.

The Corcoran Gallery, inspired by the collection of American paintings owned
by Washington banker and financier William Wilson Corcoran, exhibits the work of painters
like Church, Bierstadt and Eastman Johnson in stately surroundings.
The Corcoran is also the home of one of America's most respected schools of art.

In a city of monuments, the atrium of the Grand Hyatt Washington is like a monumental city all its own.
Sunlight filters down from the sky over lush greenery and a cascading waterfall that leads to a crystal blue lagoon.
At the lagoon's edge is the Grand Cafe, where informal dining is available throughout the day. A cascade of piano
notes join the rippling of water all over the lobby forming a sensuous oasis in the center of the city.

ACCOMMODATIONS

While covering the Civil War for the Atlantic Monthly, the renowned American writer, Nathaniel Hawthorne, claimed the Willard Hotel "may be much more justly called the center of Washington and the Union than either the Capitol, the White House, or the State Department." Located on Pennsylvania Avenue, between the Capitol and the White House, the site of The Willard has served as a hotel in some form since 1816. When Henry Willard bought the property in 1850, he dreamed of creating a hotel that would attract the rich and powerful from all over the world. A star-struck Hawthorne, and others through the years, have watched that dream come true, as a long line of presidents, ambassadors, inventors and artists have mingled in the magnificent atmosphere of the hotel. The site of many important meetings and occasions, the hotel's tradition has become interwoven with the historical fabric of the city.

Two other old hotels located near the White House also have fascinating histories that rival the Willard's. The Hay-Adams, which faces St. John's Church on Lafayette Square, was built on the site of adjoining homes originally owned by famous Americans Henry Adams and John Hay. Medici tapestries from the 17th century adorn the warm walnut walls of the lobby at the Hay-Adams, and some of its finest rooms overlook the White House, past the Washington and Jefferson monuments, to the glimmering waters of the Potomac River in the distance. The Sheraton Carlton, a few blocks north on 16th Street, reflects the grace and grandeur of an Italian Renaissance palace with elegantly understated rooms and one of the District's most acclaimed restaurants, Allegro. With hand carved mahogany woodwork and Italian marble floors, Allegro offers sophisticated dining for even the most demanding connoisseurs.

Classic does not necessarily mean old, though. More recent additions to the city's landscape include hotels like the Capital Hilton, the Park Hyatt, the Four Seasons and the Washington Court, where "classic" service and style go hand in hand. The Capital Hilton, located on the famous 16th Street corridor, offers winding staircases and richly crafted details that create intimate atmospheres despite the capacity to accommodate large groups and conventions. And the Washington Court, with a view of the Capitol from practically every angle, welcomes visitors with a spectacular marble and glass lobby that conveys the hotel's commitment to classic services in a contemporary setting.

Other contemporary "classic" hotels include the Hyatt Regency on Capitol Hill, the J.W. Marriott and the Holiday Inn Crowne Plaza at Metro Center. The Hyatt Regency on Capitol Hill offers accommodations for even the hardest to please, with several restaurants that cater to any mood. The Capitol View Club, located on the top floor of the hotel, looks out on historic Capitol Hill and a stunning view of the Capitol building. The J.W. Marriott is located at National Place, one of Washington's most popular shopping areas. In the same block as the National Theatre and the Warner Theatre, one can walk from the J.W. Marriott to any number of performances in minutes. The Holiday Inn Crowne Plaza is just around the corner from the Washington Convention Center, as well as the Metro Center, the hub of the city's bright new subway system. Majestic in appearance, the Crowne Plaza invokes the finest accommodations the city has to offer.

With convention business and tourism booming over the past few years, the District has witnessed the construction of several huge hotels that can accommodate the influx of business people and tourist groups who have recently discovered the city's pleasures. The Grand Hyatt Washington is one of these hotels. In a city of monuments, the Grand Hyatt's atrium lobby is a monument in itself. Twelve stories high, and enclosed by glass, sunlight filters down from the sky over greenery and cascading water that form a lush lagoon at the center of the hotel. The Ramada Renaissance Hotel-Techworld, like the Grand Hyatt, is located near the Convention Center. Also on the edge of Chinatown, its lobby highlights oriental art in a setting that includes a grand pagoda. Connected with the Techworld Plaza, a mammoth multi-use complex of offices and retail space, the hotel offers a wide array of services. Also part of Techworld Plaza is Tech 2000, the world's first museum of interactive multimedia exhibits, with displays on computers and communications technology.

Away from the center of town, on the Connecticut Avenue corridor, are the city's two largest hotels. The Washington Hilton Hotel and Towers is a huge, curving structure that provides conference rooms for groups of any magnitude. Their patio and pool area is like a quiet oasis of greenery in the city atmosphere. And their famous International Ballroom, the largest ballroom in the city, has been the location of many memorable events.

The Sheraton Washington, the largest hotel in Washington, D.C., has over 1500 rooms. Walking through its lobbies, halls and corridors is a fascinating experience. Something is always happening here, whether it is the bright lights of a news conference, or the reception of a foreign entourage. With ballroom facilities and thousands of square feet of conference space, the Sheraton Washington can handle practically any occasion.

One section of the city that is going through significant changes is the area a few blocks south of the National Mall. At L'Enfant Plaza, the Loews L'Enfant Plaza Hotel stands at the center of a complex of shopping and office space that seems to embrace constant movement. Within walking distance of many government departments, as well as the Mall and an array of attractions along the Washington Channel, Loews L'Enfant Plaza Hotel is built on top of a Metro Station that allows easy access to the entire city.

Just a block south of the National Air and Space Museum is the Holiday Inn Capitol. Designed to accommodate business and tourist groups in sizes from the modest to the substantial, the Holiday Inn Capitol is within blocks of the Capitol building, congressional offices, government agencies, as well as all the enticements on the Mall. Like the Loews L'Enfant, the Holiday Inn Capitol is also within walking distance of the Washington Channel, where one can visit tour boats, restaurants on the water and a wide array of attractions that are making the area south of the Mall one of the District's brightest new fun spots.

Washington, D.C. is a hotbed for tourism and business, and the city's accommodations offer unique choices and spectacular services that make any visit to the District a delightful occasion.

Techworld Plaza, located in the heart of the flourishing East End, is strategically positioned
in the center of the office market between the U.S. Capitol and the White House. Four interconnected buildings
make up Techworld Plaza: three house office and retail space and the fourth is the Ramada Renaissance Hotel.
Amenities abound at Techworld, with restaurants, retail shops, a health club, Tech 2000 – a multi-media gallery –
and a fun and exciting landscaped pedestrian plaza with authentic Chinese gardens.

The Ramada Renaissance Hotel-Techworld, one of the city's premiere convention hotels,
is the 15-story, 800-room flagship hotel of Ramada International Hotels and Resorts.
Directly across the street from the Convention Center, and on the edge of historic Chinatown,
the hotel has created a unique lobby setting that includes Chinese gardens and a pagoda. Within steps of Metro
Center and a host of museums and galleries, the Ramada Renaissance boasts one of the best locations in town.

With the meticulous restoration of the Willard Inter-Continental Hotel,
guests feel as if they have stepped back into history. For its century-long tradition of hosting
American presidents, the old Willard was known as the "residence of presidents." The Main Lobby of the
Willard Inter-Continental has reclaimed its historic role as the place to see and be seen in Washington.

Located one block from the White House, the Willard Inter-Continental Hotel has often
been known as "the crown jewel of Pennsylvania Avenue." The award-winning hotel offers convenient
access to the Capitol and other government buildings, the business and diplomatic communities,
as well as all tourist and cultural attractions.

Enjoy a breathtaking view of the U.S. Capitol from atop the Hyatt Regency Washington Hotel
at the Capitol View Club. The Capitol building, bathed in white light, casts a perfect spell for an
unforgettable dinner in the heart of Washington. The restaurant features fine American cuisine.
There is also an adjoining lounge for sunset cocktails.

Located just blocks from the Capitol, Supreme Court and the Library of Congress,
the Hyatt Regency Washington on Capitol Hill is also within minutes of Washington's famous museums,
monuments and historic sites. With over 800 rooms, health club and pool, and one of the city's largest
meeting facilities, the Hyatt Regency Washington is ideal for business travelers,
meetings or leisure visits to the Nation's Capital.

Dining in the English country estate setting of the John Hay Room,
in the Hay-Adams Hotel, is like visiting Washington during an earlier era. Built on the site of adjoining homes
owned by John Hay and Henry Adams, the Hay-Adams offers a respite from the modern atmosphere of the city.
Located on Lafayette Square, and looking out over the White House, the presence of times past
can be felt among the richly restored rooms and elegantly appointed surroundings.

Located across the street from the Convention Center, with ballrooms and banquet rooms
to accommodate any size meeting, the Grand Hyatt Washington provides a wide range of services
for convention and business travelers. With direct underground access to Metro Center and
within walking distance of dozens of museums, monuments and galleries, the Grand Hyatt Washington is
central to the city's attractions, making a stay here convenient and memorable.

The traditional feel of Wardman Tower, combined with the contemporary atmosphere
of the hotel's main building, gives expression to the wealth of options that the Sheraton Washington offers.
Wardman Tower boasts beautiful suites that overlook the wooded neighborhoods of Woodley Park.
The main building contains nearly 1,500 rooms, as well as an amazing
assortment of convention and function facilities.

With over 1,500 rooms between two buildings, the Sheraton Washington is the largest hotel in the city.
Located near the National Zoo, just off Connecticut Avenue, the Sheraton is like a fascinating indoor city,
where the sounds and sites of banquets, news conferences and important meetings seem to fill
every room and hallway. With ballroom and conference space available for even the largest meetings,
the Sheraton is a favorite with conventions and large groups.

Located just two blocks from the White House, on the historic 16th Street corridor,
The Capital Hilton offers intimate space for individuals and small groups, as well as larger meeting rooms and
function halls for groups and conventions. Filled with winding staircases and contemporary art work,
The Capital Hilton extends to its visitors the "classic" hotel tradition of luxury, comfort and service,
in a location that is central to all of Washington's important addresses.

Designed to resemble an Italian Renaissance palace, The Carlton, an ITT Sheraton Luxury Hotel,
recently completed a $20 million renovation which restored it to its original grandeur. Established in 1926,
and located just two blocks from the White House on 16th Street, The Carlton has long been
an historic favorite for Washington dignitaries. With 197 elegantly appointed guest rooms,
one of Washington's most acclaimed restaurants, Allegro, and a lush garden terrace,
The Carlton has become renowned for its unparalleled service and distinguished style.

Being near every major tourist attraction on the Mall is just part of the convenience of the
Holiday Inn Capitol. Facilities at the hotel include an exercise room, restaurants that cater to any mood,
meeting rooms for all occasions and a rooftop pool that overlooks the city. The hotel is also just north of the
Washington Channel, where a romantic setting of sailboats and fine restaurants is just moments away.

The Holiday Inn Capitol is located only one block south of the National Air & Space Museum,
and within walking distance of every monument and museum on the Mall. Also surrounded by the offices of
dozens of federal departments and agencies, as well as just six blocks from the Capitol and congressional offices,
the Holiday Inn Capitol is ideal for those touring the town or for those here on business.

Step into the sweeping, spacious lobby of the Loews L'Enfant Plaza Hotel,
where the finest appointments convey the sense of pride the hotel takes in its service and
convenience to the city. Located just blocks from the National Mall and all of the major Smithsonian museums,
many of the 372 rooms at L'Enfant Plaza Hotel offer beautiful views of the Potomac River,
Capitol Hill and the National Monuments on the Mall.

Centered in the ever expanding L'Enfant Plaza, practically a city within the city,
the Loews L'Enfant Plaza Hotel is within walking distance of major government departments and offices,
an underground shopping promenade and an 800 seat theatre. And since it is located directly above one of
Washington's largest Metro stops, every other attraction in and around the city is just minutes away.

Located in the heart of Capitol Hill, and blocks from the Capitol building,
the Washington Court Hotel is at the center of the excitement that is Washington. Along with its ideal location,
the Washington Court offers excitement on its own, with function rooms, large ballrooms and
hospitality suites that are perfect for intimate receptions as well as larger meetings and banquets.

In the expansive, four-story lobby at the Washington Court Hotel,
you feel the luxurious atmosphere that the hotel projects. Brightly lit marble bestows the hotel with a
sense of the European, while the elegantly appointed rooms lend a sense of intimacy and comfort that is
welcome after a long day of seeing the sites or meeting appointments.

The J.W. Marriott Hotel is the flagship hotel for the Marriott Corporation.
Located on the historic Pennsylvania Avenue corridor, two blocks from the White House, the J.W. Marriott is
at the center of some of Washington's finest shopping areas and within walking distance of the National and
Warner theatres. A few blocks from the Convention Center, the Marriott has 772 luxurious rooms, and is
large enough to handle convention-sized groups, yet noted for its impeccable services and amenities.

The Holiday Inn Crowne Plaza at Metro Center is set in the heart of Washington's revitalized Downtown area.
One block from the D.C. Convention Center and within walking distance of many federal agencies,
the Crowne Plaza is central to much of the city's commercial and convention interests.
For leisure travelers, the Crowne Plaza is just blocks from the White House, the Mall and fine theatres,
shops and restaurants. The hotel is located on top of the hub of the Metro subway system,
making any other location in or around the city a short ride away.

This romantic pool setting at the Washington Hilton is just four blocks from Dupont Circle
in the heart of Washington. Spread over seven acres, the Washington Hilton and Towers is a unique downtown
convention and resort hotel, offering pool, tennis courts and a new spa providing a full range of services.
The Hilton has 1,123 guest rooms, 82 suites and 32 function rooms, several of which open directly
onto the Gazebo gardens and swimming pool patio.

The extraordinary International Ballroom at the Washington Hilton and Towers is an architectural wonder.
The scene for a variety of gatherings, including Presidential inaugural balls, state banquets and gala benefits,
the ballroom is the largest in Washington. Although the International Ballroom seats 3,100 for banquets
and 4,200 for meetings, a raised mezzanine and an absence of columns means that
even at full capacity, there is no such thing as a bad seat.

Part of Washington's recent redevelopment has been spurred by increased interest in tourism and convention business. The Washington Convention Center, opened in 1983, has fueled that development by offering space for a multitude of conventions and trade shows. Hundreds of thousands of conventioneers visit the city every year to do business and enjoy the sites the District has to offer.

From flower shows to huge business meetings, the Washington Convention Center
can accommodate gatherings of any size and interest. Located on 9th Street and New York Avenue,
the Convention Center has stimulated tourist and commercial growth throughout the city.
By creating a new interest in tourism, the Convention Center has led to the development of many grand hotels
and fine restaurants that accommodate the growing number of visitors coming to the city.

The Capitol is the focal point of the legislative branch of the Federal government.
From the steps at the west entrance, members of Congress sometimes address the press after newsmaking
sessions. As they do, they gaze westward to the nation's monuments and memorials and are reminded
of the great men and women who have served the nation before them.

FEDERAL GOVERNMENT

Standing on the steps of the Capitol, one can gaze west across the Mall and see people engaged in a myriad of leisure activities. Families, maps and souvenirs in hand, cross the Mall in search of museums; joggers and bicyclists work across 3rd Street and turn up Jefferson Drive toward the Washington Monument. On the lawns of the Mall, kids throw frisbees and footballs while couples spread blankets for late afternoon picnics in summer.

Inside the Capitol, there are thousands of others absorbed in different activities: endeavors that shape the lives of everyone in the nation and the world. The home of our Federal government, Washington, D.C. accommodates a complex network of agencies and departments that comprise the three branches of government – the legislative, the judicial and the executive.

The Capitol building is the center of the legislative branch. Inside, grand, domed chambers for the Senate and the House of Representatives are connected by a series of spectacularly ornate corridors and hallways. In the constant commotion of congressmen and -women, pages and staff, lobbyists and speakers, this is where laws are formed and adopted. The mood here is somber and serious, yet accessibility is remarkably open, just as the founding fathers had planned.

Within walking distance of the Capitol are six congressional office buildings, three each for the Senate and the House. Named for prominent senators and representatives, the offices are all linked to the Capitol by subways that allow for rapid access. The Capitol grounds are as impressive as the interior of the Capitol itself. Designed by Frederick Law Olmsted, the landscape architect of New York's Central Park, the grounds include wide-open lawns and sheltered grottos that create a tranquil atmosphere amid the often frantic pace of Congress.

Directly east of the Capitol, among beautifully maintained lawns and cherry trees, is the Supreme Court – the center of the judicial branch. For years, the Justices of the Supreme Court had convened in the Capitol building. In 1935, the Court moved to its present home, in the huge neoclassical structure that conveys the strength and dignity that the Court maintains. Inside, visitors are welcome to peruse a number of historical exhibits, as well as sit in on the traditional open sessions when the Justices hear cases. Beyond this, much of the work done by the Supreme Court is protected by a veil of secrecy and detachment. Working in richly appointed suites, Justices have ample staff to do research and carry out the production and printing of Court decisions. Each Justice also tends to the business of one or more of the thirteen federal circuits.

Although almost everyone is aware that the White House is the centerpiece of the third branch of government, the executive, the offices of a multitude of executive departments and agencies are spread throughout the city. For example, to the west of the White House stands the gigantic Old Executive Office Building. Built in French Second Empire style, the building was constructed to house a growing executive staff. Commissioned in 1871, the ostentatious structure, for years considered gaudy and monstrous, took seventeen years to complete.

Across Pennsylvania Avenue stands a more humble edifice: the Blair House. Once the home of journalist Francis Blair, the house now acts as the official guest quarters for visiting heads of state. President Truman lived here while the White House was being renovated during the late 1940's and early '50's.

To the east of the White House is the Treasury Department, a huge Greek Revival structure that some claim was built by President Jackson to block his view from foes in Congress. Begun in 1836, the Treasury Department building took over thirty years to complete.

Many of the departments and agencies of the executive branch are located south and east of the White House, in an area known as the Federal Triangle. Begun in the late 1920's, and continued through the Great Depression of the '30's, the Federal Triangle contains many low-level, neoclassical-style buildings that include the Commerce and Justice Departments, the Internal Revenue Service, the National Archives, the Interstate Commerce Commission and the Federal Trade Commission. Although the buildings in the area maintain a level of architectural consistency, many offer fascinating details that make each building unique. For example, the Commerce has beautiful mosaic floors, and the Justice extends examples of Art Deco designs that make each a fascinating individual structure.

To the west of the White House, more departments dot the landscape. The Interior Department, the State Department, the Office of Personal Management and the Federal Reserve Board are all established in this area. South of the White House, overlooking the Tidal Basin, is the Bureau of Engraving and Printing. One of Washington's most fascinating attractions, this is where paper money and stamps are printed.

More recently, office buildings for executive departments and agencies have been located south of the Mall, below Independence Avenue. Most notable is the Department of Agriculture, an enormous structure that fills an entire two block area from 12th to 14th Streets, and even reaches over Independence and along Jefferson Drive. Other departments in this area, in and around the recently renovated L'Enfant Plaza, include the Department of Education, the Environmental Protection Agency, the Department of Transportation, Health and Human Services, Housing and Urban Development and the National Aeronautics and Space Administration.

Away from the center of the District is the Pentagon, which is virtually a city in itself. The familiar five-sided structure has its own dispensary, post office and fire department. And, despite its size, no two points are more than a seventeen minute walk apart.

Northwest of the city, shrouded in the shadowy woods of Langley, Virginia, is the headquarters of the Central Intelligence Agency, which is part of the Defense Department. Established in 1947, the C.I.A. serves as the center of international intelligence.

While the Pentagon and the C.I.A. are concerned with foreign security, the Federal Bureau of Investigation serves to avert potential threats from within the nation. A huge new headquarters was completed for the F.B.I. in the mid-seventies, and tours there include popular displays on gangsters, marksmanship and exhibits relating to the history of the Bureau.

Also located in Washington, D.C., and an integral part of the nation's business, are embassies and associations. There are over 2200 diplomatic representatives in the city, representing over 150 nations. Embassies include many beautiful traditional mansions, like the British Embassy, as well as newer, dramatic structures like the $30 million Canadian Chancery. The Canadian Chancery even contains its own art gallery and theater.

With political influence so intensely concentrated in the city, many national associations have located their headquarters in Washington. Lobbyists from a number of interests exert the views of their constituents on members of Congress and the executive branch. Other administrative and lobbying organizations, like the National Institutes of Science, are also located in the District.

The Federal government is full of interesting details and history. Spread in and around the city, many departments offer fascinating tours and exhibits that should not be missed.

Within the halls and chambers of the Capitol, bills are formed, debated and passed into law.
Originally designed in the 1790's, the Capitol has expanded to include enlarged wings for the House and Senate,
as well as six Congressional office buildings. The offices are connected to the Capitol by
underground passageways that facilitate easy access.

Although security is doggedly maintained, the Capitol and Congressional offices are
remarkably accessible so that constituents and lobbyists can make their opinions known.
The Capitol is also a popular tourist attraction, with the Rotunda and Statuary Hall
being two of the most fascinating sites in the entire city.

From its huge marbled columns on the outside, to its richly furnished corridors and chambers inside,
the Supreme Court projects an air of assured dignity and strength. The center of the judicial branch, the Court's
nine justices work in a setting that is protective and somewhat secretive. Located here since 1935,
the Supreme Court had previously convened in the Capitol.

The massive structure of the Supreme Court sits among wide lawns with flowering trees and bushes.
Across the street from the Capitol, the site originally contained the Old Capitol Prison. Inside its huge bronzed
doors, legislation is upheld or repealed by the decision of the court's nine justices.

Blair House

White House

White House

Old Executive Office Building

The White House, originally called the President's House, is the centerpiece of the executive branch of the Federal government. The Blair House, across the street, acts as the official guest quarters for visiting heads of state. The gigantic Old Executive Office Building was begun in 1871 in order to house the offices of a growing executive staff. It took seventeen years to complete.

Sitting in the center of eighteen acres of gardens, green lawns and modest fountains,
the White House is one of Washington's most recognized symbols. This view, from the south,
shows off the simplicity of design that has survived many changes and expansions since it was designed
by James Hoban in 1797. The White House is the oldest public building in Washington.

Bureau of Engraving and Printing

Department of the Treasury

Bureau of Engraving and Printing

Bureau of Engraving and Printing

Part of the Department of the Treasury, the Bureau of Engraving and Printing is one
of the most visited sites in the city. And it's no wonder. It is here that paper money, postage stamps,
bonds and certificates are produced. Tours show the complex intaglio process of making currency,
from engraving and inking, to checking for defects and stacking.

Internal Revenue Service

Federal Reserve Board

Federal Trade Commission

Department of Commerce

Four Federal departments involved with money and trade include the Internal Revenue Service, Federal Reserve, Federal Trade Commission and the Department of Commerce. The Department of Commerce building, which occupies two blocks on the east side of the Ellipse, has unique mosaic floors that distinguishes it from other departments in the Federal Triangle.

Department of Justice

J. Edgar Hoover Building, F.B.I.

Department of State

U.S. Information Agency

Departments and agencies have spread throughout the city as the executive branch
has steadily expanded since World War I. The State Department occupies a huge structure in Foggy Bottom;
the Justice Department is part of the Federal Triangle dating to Roosevelt's New Deal era. The J. Edgar Hoover
Building was part of the Pennsylvania Avenue revitalization that began in the 1970's.
The U.S. Information Agency is located in the growing area south of the Mall.

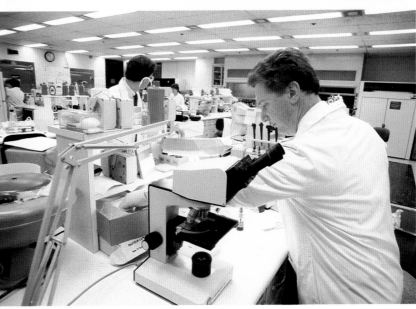

In the offices and computer rooms of the FBI building, highly trained agents
utilize high-tech equipment to study identification photos, bloodstains and other evidence in order
to protect the nation from crimes of national scope. Tours will take visitors through exhibits
of FBI history and end with a fascinating firearms demonstration.

Department of Housing and Human Development

Department of Transportation

Department of Health and Human Services

Department of Education and NASA

During the Sixties and early Seventies, many federal departments and agencies moved into the area
south of the Mall. Among the modern architecture here are two structures designed by architect Marcel Breuer:
the Department of Housing and Urban Development building and the Hubert H. Humphrey building, which
houses the Department of Health and Human Services. The Department of Transportation, NASA
and Department of Education are also located in this area.

112

Department of Labor

Department of Agriculture

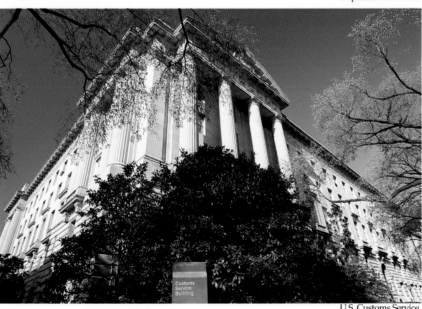

U.S. Customs Service

Department of the Interior

The Department of the Interior building was constructed during Roosevelt's New Deal era, and it includes social-realist art that was prevalent at that time. The huge structure housing the Department of Agriculture stretches two blocks along and across Independence Avenue on the south side of the Mall. The Department of Labor is located near the Capitol, just outside of the Federal Triangle. The U.S. Customs Service is in the Federal Triangle.

National Academy of Sciences

Library of Congress

U. S. Court House

Map Room at Library of Congress

The statue of Albert Einstein, at the National Academy of Sciences, is one of hundreds
of statues spread throughout the city, as well as one of the most unique. The Library of Congress is the
world's largest library, with over 532 miles of shelving space, including some used specifically for maps.
The U.S. Court House, near the Capitol, is where most federal trials are held.

Greek Embassy

British Embassy

Canadian Embassy

Pan American Union

Nearly 150 countries are represented in Washington by over 2,200 diplomats,
making the city the international center of the nation. Many of the embassies, like the British Embassy,
are located in palatial mansions along Embassy Row. Others are spread throughout town, like the
Canadian Embassy, a huge contemporary structure that includes a public art gallery and theatre.
The Pan American Union is located on Constitution Avenue, just west of the White House.

Washington's beloved football team, the Redskins, play before riotous fans at the
Robert F. Kennedy Stadium in the fall and winter. Perennial playoff contenders, the National Football League
franchise plays in one of professional football's most competitive divisions. They are more than
up to the task, though, having won the Super Bowl in 1983 and 1988.

SPORTS AND RECREATION

Whether you want to cheer for your favorite team from the stands, or you crave hitting the streets to work up a little sweat on your own, Washington, D.C. has the resources available for almost any form of sport and recreational activity.

Washington's professional sports history is filled with stories of glory and legend. The city's pro football franchise, the Redskins, has been one of the most successful National Football League teams in recent years. Perennial playoff contenders, the Redskins play in one of the most competitive divisions in professional sports, the Eastern Division of the National Football Conference. The "Skins" have thrived on the challenge; Washington football fans have celebrated two recent Super Bowl championships with the team, in 1983 and 1988.

And what fans the Redskins have. The only way one can get tickets to a regular-season game is to know the owner, or maybe curry favor with a season-ticket holder. Every game is a sell-out, and it's been that way for years. If you're fortunate enough to be one of the 55,000 to make it into Robert F. Kennedy Stadium on game day, you know that the Redskins put on a show that has zealots romping and stomping in the stands. If you're not fortunate enough to have a season ticket, check out one of the exhibition games at the stadium in August.

Things also get pretty wild at the Capital Centre, the state-of-the-art arena where the Washington Bullets play professional basketball. Members of the National Basketball Association, the Bullets transported their electrifying brand of round-ball to D.C. in 1973. During nearly two decades of play here, the Bullets have captured playoff spots in almost every season. In 1978, they battled the Seattle Supersonics in a thrilling seven-game series and earned their only championship in franchise history. Currently coached by former-Bullet all-star Wes Unseld, the team is in a rebuilding phase. However, Unseld's team has turned more than a few heads during the past few years with a style of play that local fans have fallen in love with.

Another professional team that calls the Capital Centre home is the Capitals. The hockey franchise, formed in 1973, has earned a spot in the playoffs each year since the 1982-1983 season. With the help of choice draft picks and increased fan support, the "Caps" have improved steadily from year to year. Over the last few seasons, they've sold out almost half of their games, and new fans are discovering that the game is fast-paced and incredibly fun to watch. With the team's winning tradition, the coveted Calder Cup Trophy, the symbol of the National Hockey League's champion, seems to be just on the horizon.

Local colleges and universities also offer exciting action in the local sports scene. The Georgetown Hoyas are celebrated across the country for their rough and tough style of basketball play that has taken them to the NCAA's Final Four on several occasions. The Terrapins, from the University of Maryland, regularly field nationally competitive teams in basketball, football and lacrosse, just to name a few.

In recent years, an enormously popular fitness craze has swept through the nation. Luckily, the District has recreational options available that cater to every interest. With park land spread throughout the city, anything is possible, from jogging and hiking to biking, boating and golf.

During the eighties, thousands discovered that Washington is a runner's paradise. It seems as though every path, every street, is a potential Shangri-la for runners who want to enjoy the multitude of sites in the city. One of the most preferred areas to run is along the Mall. Encircled by a soft gravel path that stretches over three miles, the Mall's flat, wide course follows a tree-lined route past monuments, museums and galleries. Long distance runners, bikers and hikers favor a variety of paths in and around Rock Creek Park and Mount Vernon. Biking has been a cherished pastime in D.C. for over a century, and the quality of the District's bike paths have kept pace with advances in cycling equipment over the past few decades. A great way to get exercise, many have discovered that biking is also one of the premiere ways to tour the city.

Another favorite area for biking and running is along the C&O Canal towpath. Here, devotees may commence in Georgetown and work a course that reaches as far as thirteen miles along a gorgeous natural setting. Shorter runs are available along the Hains Point Loop, at East Potomac Park along the Washington Channel.

In addition to biking and running, East Potomac Park offers a thirty-six hole golf course that is open year round. Owned by the Park Service, and accessible to the public, the East Potomac Park course is one of two public golf courses in Washington. The other course, the Rock Creek Golf Course, is located on 16th and Rittenhouse Street, N.W., near the National Zoo. The Rock Creek course is an eighteen-hole course and is also open year round.

Rock Creek Park also offers a superb setting for horseback riding, which is available at the Rock Creek Park Horse Center. Here, trail and pony rides will lead you on leisurely expeditions through the lush atmosphere of Rock Creek Park. If your riding mood tends to the more competitive, check out one of the Polo clubs around town. Polo on the Mall is a tradition in the city that goes back for years, and spectators will tell you it's as much fun to watch as it is to play.

For those feeling land-locked, Washington has exciting choices for a multitude of water sports. Rowboats and canoes are available at several locations in the city for recreational use on the Potomac. Sailboat rentals are available from April to October at the Washington Sailing Marina, just south of National Airport.

Furthermore, the Potomac River is a major tributary of the famous Chesapeake Bay. Washington is just one of many convenient stopping points for boaters working their way up or down the bay. A short car or boat ride away, the Chesapeake Bay is world renowned for its yachting, sailing, fishing and crabbing.

A common sight along the Potomac, on the Georgetown Channel, are racing skulls, or shells. These sleek racing boats are custom-built for either individuals or teams, and several area universities and high schools field teams that race along the Potomac in both the spring and fall. Most of the excitement is centered at the Harry T. Thompson Boat Center, located on the Georgetown Channel.

Ice skating is also available at several locations around town, with one of the most popular being the Sculpture Garden Ice Rink. Located between the National Gallery of Art and the Museum of Natural History, the rink is open daily from mid-November through mid-March.

Still more is available for health and fitness enthusiasts in the city. One can work out practically anywhere in Washington, since most hotels now have their own spas and health clubs. In addition, the city is full of courts and fields for tennis, basketball and touch football. There are an abundance of clubs and neighborhood recreation centers that make activities available on a assortment of levels.

Whether you want to watch some of the finest professional or collegiate competition in the world, or you want to spend a lazy weekend afternoon tossing a frisbee around on the Mall, Washington has a plethora of resources available for any sport or activity.

The Washington Bullets basketball team moved into the state-of-the-art Capital Centre in 1973.
Since then, they have racked up dozens of playoff appearances, and they won the National Basketball
Association's Championship during the 1977-1978 season. The Bullets are currently in a rebuilding phase,
but the young team has turned more than a few heads under the guidance of former Bullet all-star Wes Unseld.

Washington may be south of the Canadian border, but locals have discovered
that the Washington Capitals hockey team can put on a pretty exciting display of skating and stickwork.
The National Hockey League franchise, formed in 1973, has steadily improved since its first playoff appearance
in 1983, and the Calder Cup Championship Trophy appears to be increasingly within the team's grasp.

Rowing

Team Rowing

Jogging

Boating at Georgetown Harbor

With miles of paths, roadways and waterways, as well as acres of undisturbed parkland, Washington, D.C. is a perfect place for all kinds of recreational activity. Over the last decade, joggers have become a permanent part of the city's landscape, and boaters of all kinds are frequently sighted in the marinas and channels located along the Potomac River.

The water of the Potomac River sparkles at sunset as a local rowing team practices into the evening.
Racing shells, or skulls, like this one, are sleek and fast as they effortlessly glide across the water.
Teams from Georgetown and George Washington Universities, as well as Trinity College and
several high schools race along the Potomac at the Georgetown Channel.

Capitol Hill is a sophisticated neighborhood of brick row homes and well-kept gardens.
Markets, fine restaurants and grassy squares share space here with the Supreme Court, the Library of Congress
and the Folger Shakespeare Library and Theatre. The Capitol dome looms over the neighborhood
from Jenkins' Hill, the highest elevation in the city.

NEIGHBORHOODS

Washington, D.C. is an international city where many different cultures weave a complex patchwork of neighborhoods, each with its own characteristic flair and history, into a tapestry that makes up the District. A walk through Washington's neighborhoods proposes a rich variety of unique lifestyles, as well as an engrossing historical overview of the city's development since Scottish immigrants first settled in Georgetown in the early 18th century.

Of all the District's neighborhoods, Georgetown is the oldest and most historic. After the Revolutionary War, George Washington is reported to have visited with Pierre L'Enfant in a Georgetown tavern, where they discussed their ambitious plans for the city. Today, Georgetown's restaurants and saloons are still a favorite enticement among weary travellers. Also popular are a vast assortment of antique shops, galleries and stores lining the sidewalks of M Street and Wisconsin, that lure visitors into the heart of the neighborhood. Settled in the early 1800's, when the Beall family built a plantation in the area, the neighborhood is bordered at the south by the Potomac River and the C&O Canal, where hiking, jogging and biking are among the preferred pastimes. After years of restoration, Georgetown retains the enchanting atmosphere of times gone by, with narrow, tree-lined streets featuring historic homes of Georgian, Federal and Victorian character.

Like Georgetown, Capitol Hill is another captivating neighborhood abundant with historic sites, beautiful homes and famous eateries. Originally named Goose Creek, then Tiber and Jenkins' Hill, Capitol Hill sits at the city's highest elevation, what L'Enfant called "a pedestal waiting for a monument." In the shadow of the Capitol, restaurants and bars brim with Congressional staff and lobbyists as they discuss politics over coffee or a sandwich. Elegant brick townhomes sit among national treasures, like the Library of Congress, the Folger's Library and Theatre, and the Supreme Court.

Moving north and west of the Capitol is Washington's most rapidly changing neighborhood, Downtown. Dominated by Pennsylvania Avenue, Downtown is the city's business and shopping district. From 10th to 14th Streets, some of Washington's finest stores and shopping malls are located. Moving further west, across K Street, and almost as far as Georgetown, are the mid-rise office buildings that signal the rapidly expanding business facets of the city. A development boom has touched this part of the neighborhood, and each trip one makes into town will reveal something new. Recently, older structures have been torn down to make way for newer, more modern office buildings. The pace in the streets here is rapid, as the sidewalks bulge with business-suited workers at mid-day, rushing to and fro in search of a quick lunch or their next appointment.

Just east of Downtown, around 7th to 9th Streets, is Chinatown. In this richly ethnic neighborhood, visitors are greeted by bold colors and fine restaurants. The streets here come alive with activity and excitement when residents celebrate the Chinese New Year with vibrant parades and celebrations.

Washington's most ethnically diverse neighborhood is Adams Morgan, located northwest of the White House at 18th and Columbia. Mostly Latin, the neighborhood embraces diplomats, artists and new immigrants. A variety of ethnic restaurants stand side by side here, offering a cornucopia of culinary delights. On Saturdays, open-air markets attract a vast array of nationalities, and a spirited feeling fills the air as one strolls the festive streets, window-shopping and people-watching.

Just south and west of Adams Morgan is Dupont Circle, an historic and vibrant neighborhood centered by a park honoring Union Admiral Samuel Francis Dupont. Considered Washington's Greenwich Village, the neighborhood is bursting with fine shops and restaurants. Dupont Circle is also the best place to catch street artists entertaining or practicing their crafts. It also boasts many of the city's most beautiful historic homes, including Woodrow Wilson's home, where he retired after serving as president.

Another neighborhood that flaunts beautiful homes and buildings is Embassy Row, which runs along Massachusetts Avenue. This lavish neighborhood is the home of 150 foreign embassies and chanceries located in the city. A trip through the shady streets here is akin to a lesson in world affairs, with colorful flags and coats-of-arms from nations all over the world displayed proudly outside of these marvelous structures.

One of the smallest yet most historic neighborhoods in the city is Lafayette Square, located just north of the White House. This one-block square is surrounded by historic houses, like the Decatur House. The homes on the square chart the diverse architectural history of the city, and present a fascinating look at the men and women who craved the power and influence that living near the White House signified. St. John's Church is located at 15th and H Streets; it is here that every president since James Madison has worshipped. In the greenery of Lafayette Square are a number of statues honoring foreign heroes who fought in the Revolutionary War, as well as an equestrian statue of Andrew Jackson located at the center of the park.

Several blocks west of Lafayette Square is a slender strip of land, known as Foggy Bottom, that runs to the Georgetown Channel. Centered by George Washington University, and home to the Kennedy Center, Foggy Bottom is a neighborhood filled with elegant townhomes that are reminiscent of those on Capitol Hill.

Further north, away from the heart of the city, is one of Washington's more sweeping neighborhoods, Woodley Park. Near Rock Creek Park and the National Zoo, Woodley Park runs along the west side of Connecticut Avenue. Filled with homes of diverse architectural styles, the area is typified by large expanses of shaded grasses and quiet streets. The National Cathedral, just recently completed, rises majestically from the trees that spread throughout the neighborhood.

Long shadowed by the many-faceted attractions of The Mall, Washington's diverse and historic neighborhoods are experiencing a rediscovery by residents and visitors alike. Driving or walking through these neighborhoods, one can witness and participate in the activities of vital communities that are alive and thriving. Washington, D.C. is a city of cultural and historic diversity; a city where many people have joined together in a united purpose. It is a city of neighborhoods, each with its own ethnic and historic atmosphere, each open to all who have a desire to explore them.

Wisconsin Avenue is considered the heart of Georgetown's business district, where one will find unique shops and boutiques, fine restaurants, trendy bars and clubs. It is believed that George Washington and Pierre L'Enfant reviewed plans for the District 200 years ago in one of Georgetown's popular taverns.

Originally chartered in 1751 as a part of Maryland, and named George after King George II,
Georgetown is the most historic neighborhood in the District. Incorporated into Washington in 1791,
Georgetown has remained somewhat insulated from the city. It elected its own mayor until 1871 and
presently resists a Metro station in order to maintain a sense of autonomy.

125

Under the shadow of the Capitol are abundant examples of posh 19th century homes in Capitol Hill.
The neighborhood consists of a mixture of upscale three-story rowhouses, as well as smaller but elegant two-story
homes. A common touch here, among the tree-lined streets, are the splashes of color from
gardens planted and maintained by the area's proud residents.

Along with its elegant ambience, Capitol Hill is famous for its restaurants, cafes and bars.
It is here that congressional staff and lobbyists gather, after long and hectic days,
to casually discuss the business of the nation.

Dupont Circle

Foggy Bottom

Dupont Circle

Dupont Circle

Considered Washington's Greenwich Village, Dupont Circle is a highlight for those with an interest
in the arts. Beautifully preserved homes share the area with a number of galleries, cafes and specialty stores.
Named for Admiral Samuel Francis Dupont in 1884, the neighborhood dates to a time of
great expansion that occurred after the Civil War.

Foggy Bottom earned its name from the swampland and river mists that were
prominent when it was the site of many of the area's factories and breweries. Today, Foggy Bottom is one
of Washington's most prestigious neighborhoods and is the home of the impressive State Department,
the Kennedy Center, the elegant Watergate complex and George Washington University.

Lafayette Square is one of the most historic areas in the city. Across G Street from the White House, the square is packed with historic sites, like the Decatur House. St. John's Church, known as the "Church of the Presidents," is located here, and the famous equestrian statue of Andrew Jackson stands at the center of Lafayette Park.

Pennsylvania Avenue, called "America's Main Street," is the major thoroughfare running
through the heart of Downtown Washington. Major renovations here, begun in the 1960's, have created
a stunning reversal of fortunes for this exciting area. Home to the Federal Triangle, Downtown offers
some of the finest shopping in D.C., as well as some of its most developed commercial spaces.

131

Currently the "hippest" neighborhood in the District, Adams Morgan is a collection of
diverse political personalities and international cultures. Eclectic shops and restaurants of many tastes
stand side by side here. On Saturdays, the streets come alive with harmonies created
by an open air market, street vendors and musicians.

The China Friendship Archway, a gift from the People's Republic of China,
announces one's entrance into Washington's small but exuberant neighborhood of Chinatown.
Unique restaurants are in abundance here, and exhilarating parades marking the
Chinese New Year are parties that should not be missed.

133

The flags of many nations ripple in the wind along Massachusetts Avenue in a neighborhood
known as Embassy Row. Centered by Sheridan Circle, the area boasts what were once the private homes
and mansions of many of the city's prominent citizens. In the spring, many embassies open their doors
for tours to benefit local organizations.

Woodley Park

Rock Creek Park

Woodley Park

Washington Marina on Washington Channel

Areas located away from the center of town include Woodley Park, Rock Creek Park and the
Washington Channel. Woodley Park is an expansive area, near the Zoo, of large homes among tree-shaded lawns.
Rock Creek Park is a recreational paradise that stretches from Georgetown to the Maryland suburbs.
The Washington Channel, just south of the Mall, is the home of sailboats and fine restaurants.

135

Built in 1962, Dulles International Airport is considered a stunning example of modern architecture.
Its sweeping roofline, supported by dramatically angled pillars, conveys the freedom and excitement of flight.
Located on the outskirts of the city, in the Virginia suburbs, Dulles was designed by Eero Saarinen.

TRANSPORTATION

Washington, D.C. has a reputation for being a difficult town in which to travel. With its four quadrants, its circles and its diagonal streets, driving around town does certainly take some patience. But the District's reputation is largely unjustified. With a little knowledge of how the city is laid out, and with a little planning and persistence, a trip in or out of town should proceed smoothly and effortlessly.

There are three major airports that service the city, all of which are on the outskirts of town. Baltimore-Washington International Airport is the farthest from the District, located approximately 45 minutes north of Washington. Two major highways connect BWI with the Capital Beltway, which encircles the city and allows one to enter Washington from any direction. Washington is also accessible from BWI by using Amtrak rail service, cabs or buses.

West of the District, in the Virginia suburbs, is Dulles International Airport. Twenty-five miles from the city, Washington is easily approached by using the Dulles Access Road. The Access Road runs to Route 66, which enters town at the Roosevelt Memorial Bridge in Foggy Bottom.

The closest airport, National, is located just south of Washington, near Crystal City. Two major Metro lines enter Washington from National, as do buses and cabs.

Once you get near town, you might choose to use the Metro system. Opened in 1976, Metro stations are well-marked by posts topped with the letter M and the colors that designate the particular line. There are currently four lines – red, orange, blue and yellow – that reach far into the Maryland and Virginia suburbs, with dozens of stations located all over Washington. Every imaginable site in the District is within short walking distance of a Metro Station, and all metro cars and stations contain information and maps on destinations and fares.

Metro fares are based on time (rush hour is more expensive) and distance traveled. Farecards must be purchased at the station and can be added to or cashed in as one proceeds.

The subway in Washington has been a miraculous addition to the city. It is clean and timely, and it's also a good bargain for a family or group spending an entire day touring the town. Tourist passes for families or groups of four may be purchased for a full day's fare at a significant discount. Passengers can also transfer from the rail system to Metro buses within the city by using a transfer ticket, which is available at Metro Stations. The red, white and blue Metro buses are highly visible around town, and they provide service to any part of the city that is not served by a rail station.

If you decide to drive into town, you will want to familiarize yourself with the city's layout. What one must remember is that it does make sense, if you take the time to figure out the arrangement of streets and avenues.

The city is laid out in four quadrants – the Northwest, Northeast, Southwest and Southeast – so that every address in the District is followed by a NW, NE, SW, SE. The four quadrants coalesce at the Capitol Building. Because of the way the city is situated on the Potomac, most (but definitely not all) of the District's attractions are located in the northwest quadrant.

East-West streets are lettered alphabetically from the center of town out to the suburbs. There is no "J" Street since the letter J was the last letter to be added to the alphabet (some have called "J Street" the "street L'Enfant forgot."). There are also no X,Y or Z Streets. When the alphabet runs out, two syllable street names (alphabetically again: Adams, Bryant, Channing) are used, followed by three-syllable street names like Albemarle, Brandywine and Chesapeake.

North-South streets are numbered from the Capitol out and reach into the 50s. The Capitol is located, logically enough, on Capitol Street (North Capitol, South Capitol or East Capitol, depending on the direction you're heading). So, the White House is 16 blocks west of the Capitol on 1600 Pennsylvania Avenue, NW. That's 16th Street and Pennsylvania, northwest of the Capitol.

Avenues run diagonally and are named after states. There's nothing to worry about here, although you'll occasionally have to deal with one of Washington's confusing circles or squares which are often located on larger avenues. Make sure you take your time and keep your bearings by using the numbered and lettered streets that intersect avenues. That way, you can always figure out where you are.

Now you have to park. Parking around some areas of the Mall is free, but it is difficult to find spaces after early hours. Keep an eye on signs, too, because parking time is structured around rush hours. It may be alright to park in an open spot at 3:00 p.m., but you'll get towed if you haven't moved by 4:00 p.m.. Although there is some expense, it is usually easiest to find a garage and park the car for the day. Fortunately, most of what you will want to see in Washington is within walking distance, so you won't have to spend all day driving from garage to garage.

If you want to take a guided tour, there are plenty from which to choose. There are walking tours of neighborhoods, tours that highlight specific subjects, tours in foreign languages, bus tours, trolley tours, boat tours, even tours of scandals in Washington's history. The Washington, D.C. Convention and Visitors Association will be more than happy to help you choose the tour package that will best suit your needs.

Finally, a word about taxis. There are over 10,000 of them roaming the streets, so catching one won't be too difficult. The drivers understand what it's like being in a strange city, trying to find the one destination you just have to get to. Washington's cabbies are more than willing to help. Fares are based on a zone system, and maps in each cab will help you work out fares in advance.

As one may see, getting around Washington really isn't very difficult. With the Metro, tours, cabs and buses, the most laborious part of visiting Washington may be choosing which option best suits your needs.

National Airport

Tour Bus

Metro

Baltimore-Washington International Airport

Getting into and around the District is not as difficult as it may seem. Three major airports,
National, B.W.I and Dulles, service the area from around the city. In town, whether for work or pleasure,
the bright new Metro system and numerous tour and transit buses offer easy,
inexpensive options for getting anywhere in Washington.

A terminal for trains, buses and the Metro, Union Station is a unique Washington landmark
with soaring arches and gold-leaf ceilings that recall ancient Roman architecture. Recently restored, Union Station
contains over 100 specialty shops and fine restaurants in a sylvan setting of flowering bushes and trees.

The Great Falls Tavern sits along the C&O Canal in suburban Maryland,
where it now acts as a visitors center for the C&O Canal Park. Just minutes out of the city,
much of the Washington suburban area is wooded and pastoral, lending visitors and residents alike
a long list of adventurous options including hiking, bicycling and canoeing.

SURROUNDING AREAS

At the beginning of the 20th century, Washington, D.C. was still a sleepy southern town; its carefully drawn borders seemed spacious and unlimited. However, with the Federal government's tenacious growth during the years between the two World Wars, and with parallelling commercial development, the city has since strained under the restrictions of its own physical boundaries. Led by the Pentagon, a few government agencies and departments have moved or located outside of the city's limits. Furthermore, in the last few decades, many of the businesses attracted to the area for its commercial potential have located in the Virginia and Maryland suburbs. With this unprecedented growth, many suburban neighborhoods have developed, or expanded, forming one of the largest and most affluent areas in the nation.

With the Pentagon's construction during World War II, the Defense Department became one of the first federal departments to locate outside of the city's limits. In Arlington, just south of the Arlington National Cemetery, the area around the Pentagon is one of the most swiftly growing regions. Within the last few years, Pentagon City has sprung up with luxury hotels, posh residences and shopping areas. Nearby, Crystal City boasts modern-styled buildings that contain office space and shopping areas in the shadows of planes that endlessly fly in and out of Washington National Airport. Overlooking the Potomac, with a view of the District, the Northern Virginia skyline is full of sleek glass buildings with smooth lines and curving facades.

Somewhat older, but architecturally similar to Crystal City, is Rosslyn, Virginia. Crossing over the Potomac on the Roosevelt Memorial Bridge, one will pass the familiar Iwo Jima Memorial on the way into Rosslyn. As you climb the hill, the city of memorials and monuments gives way to contemporary architecture that rises high into the sky. Modern hotels, high-rise office buildings and wide boulevards are the norm here, with graceful surfaces and curving, open lines that convey the contemporary attitudes of the area's designers. Many of Washington's newer businesses are located in Rosslyn, and office workers are in abundance here, lunching in flowery alcoves and on park benches that fill the landscape under the sunny skies.

Vastly different areas than these, on the Virginia side of the Potomac, are Alexandria, McLean and Great Falls. Alexandria has a history of its own, and the area's Revolutionary-era architecture reflects its age. Down tree-lined streets and quiet avenues, Alexandria's red-brick buildings reveal charms that include unique galleries and antique shops, as well as many fine restaurants.

McLean, located north of Arlington and divided by the scenic George Washington Parkway, is a wooded area that appears more or less undisturbed from Washington's previous centuries. The Parkway is practically an attraction in itself, with extraordinary vistas overlooking the Potomac River into Georgetown and Washington. And, in the dense foliage of McLean's woods, clouded in mystery and intrigue, is the headquarters for the Central Intelligence Agency.

Driving north and west of McLean, in Great Falls, one is bound to forget that he or she is just minutes out of the traffic jams and crowds of the city. Country roads twist and turn through acres of trees that stand tall above some of the area's most handsome homes and mansions. Great Falls Park, where the rushing waters of the Potomac crash over huge, jagged rocks with deafening fury, is an attraction for anyone fascinated by the mysterious power of nature and water.

Like Virginia, the Maryland suburbs also compliment Washington's vast expansion. Bethesda, which is bordered by Wisconsin Avenue, is the home of the National Institute of Health, a huge complex that includes facilities for medical research and treatment. Also located in Bethesda is the National Naval Medical Center. An established neighborhood, Bethesda carries its age well, with beautifully tree-lined streets running through neighborhoods of distinguished brick homes. The center of town echoes Georgetown, with brick sidewalks and rows of engaging shops. Recently, the appearance of high-rise office buildings and open plazas have announced the arrival of many businesses that have discovered the pleasures of this affluent suburb northwest of the city.

Closer to the city, just east of Bethesda, is Chevy Chase. This neighborhood boasts a variety of brick, clapboard and stucco homes set among quiet streets and generous open spaces. The Columbia Country Club gives Chevy Chase an air of southern affluence that reminds one of Washington's days from the end of the 19th century.

To the northeast of the city is College Park, the home of the University of Maryland. One of the largest universities in the nation, the University of Maryland is just one of many educational facilities in the area that attract some of the finest students and professors from all over the country. Just a few miles to the north of College Park is Greenbelt, where the N.A.S.A. Goddard Flight Center and the Greenbelt Agricultural Research Center are located.

Finally, to the east of the city, just beyond Silver Hill and Camp Springs, is the Andrews Air Force Base and Naval Facility. Probably best known as the home of Air Force One, the President's official aircraft, Andrew's is a huge area that includes residential areas and facilities for those working on the base.

Washington's surrounding areas and neighborhoods, some old and some very new, offer visitors and residents an assortment of splendid sites and exciting activities within close proximity of the city. Like the city, there is a lot happening on the outskirts of town. Whether it's fine shopping along brick sidewalks you seek, a visit to an historic area, or a meandering ride over winding country roads, the Washington suburbs are brimming with exciting options just minutes from the heart of the city.

Bethesda

Andrews Air Force Base

Chevy Chase

Metro Center at Silver Spring

Washington's surrounding areas offer a variety of wonderful sites and exciting activities
within close proximity of the city. With Metro stations in many outlying neighborhoods,
one can visit areas renowned for their unique shopping, famed historic sites and
important business concerns in just a matter of minutes.

Rosslyn

Great Falls and C&O Canal

Mormon Temple in Chevy Chase

Alexandria

With surrounding areas that include the ultra-modern, as well as the historically significant,
Washington, D.C. is a city that knows no limits. Modern office buildings, dramatic temples and areas dating
to the beginning of the nation are all within minutes of the Mall. Convenient bus and
Metro routes will get you to them in minutes.

Looking from gardens at the north, the Capitol dome glows in white floodlights
that pierce the night sky. At any time of day, from any angle, the Capitol rises high above the city on Capitol Hill,
reminding all that pass by that Washington, D.C. is a vital city of symbols and remembrances.